Library of
Davidson College

Land Banking in the Control
of Urban Development

Harvey L. Flechner

The Praeger Special Studies program—utilizing the most modern and efficient book production techniques and a selective worldwide distribution network—makes available to the academic, government, and business communities significant, timely research in U.S. and international economic, social, and political development.

Land Banking in the Control of Urban Development

PRAEGER SPECIAL STUDIES IN U.S. ECONOMIC, SOCIAL, AND POLITICAL ISSUES

Praeger Publishers   New York   Washington   London

Library of Congress Cataloging in Publication Data

Flechner, Harvey L
    Land banking in the control of urban development.

    (Praeger special studies in U.S. economic, social, and political issues)
    Bibliography: p.
    1. Regional planning.   2. Metropolitan areas.
3. Land. I. Title.
HT391.F55   309.2'5'0973   74-5742
ISBN 0-275-09350-6

PRAEGER PUBLISHERS
111 Fourth Avenue, New York, N.Y. 10003, U.S.A.
5, Cromwell Place, London SW7 2JL, England

Published in the United States of America in 1974
by Praeger Publishers, Inc.

All rights reserved

© 1973 and 1974 by Harvey L. Flechner

Printed in the United States of America

Dedicated to
my wife Doll and to
my sons Jack and Michael

PREFACE

> Institutions like . . . a metropolitan land bank, which can implement metropolitan plans and can set a framework for overall metropolitan land use policies that save money and increase the institutional capacity to respond to social needs, especially those for low income groups within the metropolitan area [are], surely [a] creation that [has] to be brought forth within this decade.
>
> Charles M. Harr, <u>Wanted: Two Federal Levers for Urban Use—Land Banks and Urbank</u> (U.S. Congress, House, Committee on Banking and Currency, June 1971), p. 928.

Land banking has been proposed for many years by many and diverse sources as a necessity if metropolitan plans are to be implemented in the United States. The virtue of metropolitan land banking is seen in the taking of positive action to implement metropolitan plans as opposed to the largely restrictive or undynamic methods utilized thus far.

Public intervention in the land market is part of a natural progression of control mechanisms for plan implementation, including provision of information, location of major infrastructure elements, zoning and subdivision regulations, taxation policies, and public land acquisition. At one scale of public acquisition, for example, advance acquisition of land for public facilities, such public intervention is an aid in plan implementation but is not a major moving force in directing growth. As viewed in this study, metropolitan land banking is not simply one of a number of land-use controls. Rather, the pervasiveness of metropolitan land banking would make it the central force in implementing plans, with all other controls shaped in its support.

It is recognized by the author that a comprehensive and balanced view of the desirability of metropolitan land banking must include an examination of alternative approaches. This study does not look at alternative approaches. It serves only as an attempt to identify and examine the conceptual and practical issues of land banking on a metropolitan scale.

The overall question of alternative approaches may be viewed in terms of the following questions: Given the attainment and full coordination of all other desired land-use controls, would these be sufficient for plan implementation—and if not, is the extra increment to be gained through metropolitan land banking worth the effort? At present these questions have no answer in any but an academic sense.

Some who have looked at the problems of plan implementation have concluded that metropolitan land banking is worth the effort. This writer believes that none of the "efforts" or issues have been fully evaluated and many have not been recognized. Associated with this hypothesis is the question of whether metropolitan land banking is feasible without the attainment and coordination of additional land-use controls. This is one of the issues raised in this study.

The purpose of this study was to try to uphold or refute the hypothesis that metropolitan land banking would be an effective means for controlling metropolitan development. Evaluation of this question has been addressed at two levels. The first deals with the concept of metropolitan land banking relative to some of the existing institutional frameworks in which it would operate, such as the private land market, governmental structure, and the planning and plan implementation process.

The second level deals with the feasibility of metropolitan land banking in terms of its operational aspects. It is difficult if not unrealistic to separate these two levels in actual evaluations. Attempts have been made by the author to identify approaches to certain problems. The basic difference in the two levels is in the making of a decision by public officials in any metropolitan area to expend time and effort in taking a serious look at metropolitan land banking. If there is no recognition of the conceptual implications and agreement in principle to attempt to deal with these, then there is little hope that a metropolitan-scale land bank will be "effective" in the many ways in which that term can be viewed.

It is likely that, with the present state of our knowledge, no definitive answer can be made to the hypothesis set forth earlier. The issues raised are both fundamental and complex. For these reasons, and owing to the scope of this study in addressing the many aspects of the term "land banking," it is not possible to make an in-depth evaluation of the issues. Nevertheless, the research has been sufficient to uphold a conclusion, as will be seen in the following discussions. It is hoped that this research will lead to a better understanding of metropolitan land banking, act as an impetus for the kind of discussion that must precede serious consideration of attempting this concept in any metropolitan area, and result in a more disciplined evaluation of the operational consequences in a real context—that is, for a specific metropolitan area.

This study consists of 11 chapters. The term "land banking" has been used to describe many activities. Chapter 1 differentiates the kinds of land banking and places in context the body of the study, which addresses general land banking (defined within) at the metropolitan scale. Chapter 2 reviews the purposes of metropolitan land banking, and in Chapter 3 relationships are identified between metropolitan land banking and metropolitan plan implementation. Chapter 4 briefly raises the issue of the legality of metropolitan land banking. (Within the context of this study, its legality is not seen as an issue insofar as it affects the conceptual or practical aspects of land banking. The legality is, of course, an essential question that must be addressed before serious thought is given to applying this technique in any metropolitan area.) Chapters 5, 6 and 7 deal, respectively, with the structure of a land-bank entity, its financial aspects, and the decision process and approaches to land acquisition, holding, and disposition. Chapters 8 and 9 provide a background of U.S. and foreign experience in land banking, and Chapter 10 summarizes a number of U.S. land-banking proposals. The final chapter, 11, is a brief discussion of each of the major issues identified in this research.

This study is based largely on a review of the literature. Most of the material on this subject is very recent, having been written within the past five years. To a limited extent, informal and brief interviews (generally by telephone) have been held where it was felt that insight could be gained into the underlying reasons for certain proposals. The files were reviewed (on site) of the Baltimore Regional Planning Commission, in connection with the proposed (now existing) Baltimore Industrial Development Corporation, and of John Hansman of the Montgomery County, Maryland, Office of Planning and Capital Programming, in connection with the county's advance land-acquisition program. An interview was held with Bruce Johnson, a legislative aide to Senator Vance Hartke, concerning a related piece of legislation described in Chapter 10. Another interview was held with Krishna Murthy, assistant director of regional planning, Metropolitan Washington Council of Governments, regarding the relation of land banking to plan implementation. An interview was also held with Patrick F. Noonan, president of the Nature Conservancy, regarding financing of a land bank.

A large-scale land-banking operation has been in effect in Puerto Rico since 1962. Considering its relevance to metropolitan land banking in other parts of the United States, an extensive questionnaire was prepared and sent to the Puerto Rico Land Administration and the Puerto Rico Planning Board. Although neither agency responded, the questionnaire, which is printed in an appendix to this volume, may well serve as a useful basis for a land-banking feasibility study.

This study originated as a dissertation at the Catholic University of America for the Masters Degree in City and Regional Planning. Information and advice were obtained from a large number of sources. Published materials and interviews are acknowledged at appropriate places in the text. Thanks are extended to Julius Levine and George Oberlander, respectively adviser and reader, for their thoughtful comments and assistance. Despite this assistance, the opinions and conclusions expressed in this study, as well as any errors and omissions, are the responsibility of the author.

CONTENTS

	Page
PREFACE	vi
LIST OF TABLES	xv

PART I: THE LAND-BANKING CONCEPT

Chapter

1	DEFINITION OF LAND BANKING	3
	Project Land Banking	3
	General Land Banking	7
2	GOALS OF LAND BANKING	10
	Controlling the Urban Growth Pattern	11
	Regulating Land Price	13
	Capturing Capital Gains	14
	Regulating the Use of Land	15
	Goal Conflicts	15
	Summary	16
	Notes	17
3	RELATION TO PLAN IMPLEMENTATION	18
	Planning and Plan Implementation	18
	Land-Use Control	20
	Provision of Information	21
	Extension of Public Facilities	21
	Zoning and Subdivision Regulations	21
	Manipulation of Land Taxes	23
	Planning Improvements	24
	Improvements in Governmental Structure	24
	Summary	25
	Notes	28

Chapter		Page
4	LEGALITY OF LAND BANKING	30
	Selected Legal Opinions	30
	Eminent Domain	33
	Notes	33
5	STRUCTURE FOR LAND BANKING	35
	Governmental Levels	35
	Federal	35
	State	36
	Metropolitan	36
	Local Jurisdictions	37
	Public Corporations	37
	Other Structural Approaches	38
	Aggregation of General Land Banks	38
	Aggregation of Project Land Banks	39
	Summary	39
	Notes	40
6	FINANCING	41
	Notes	44
7	LAND ACQUISITION, HOLDING, AND DISPOSITION	45
	Market Framework	45
	Major Operational Issues	46
	How Much Land?	46
	Land Price Rise	47
	Land Taxes	48
	Equity	48
	Land Bank Decision Process	50
	Methods of Acquisition	51
	Land Holding or Management	52
	Disposition	53
	Sale Versus Lease	54
	Development Controls	55
	Disposition Price	55
	Notes	55

Chapter   Page

PART II: HISTORICAL BACKGROUND

    Introduction   59

8 THE U.S. EXPERIENCE   60

    Industrial Development   60
        Baltimore   62
        Milwaukee   63
    Advance Land Acquisition for Public Facilities   63
        Acquisition Programs   64
        Advantages and Disadvantages   66
    Urban Renewal and Housing   68
    Open Space   69
    Puerto Rico Land Administration   70
    Summary   73
    Notes   74

9 FOREIGN EXPERIENCE   76

    Comparative Experience   77
        Search   77
        Acquisition   78
        Inventory   78
        Disposition   79
        Organization   79
        Financing   80
    Notes   80

10 LAND-BANKING PROPOSALS   82

    Legislative Proposals   83
    Governmental Studies and Proposals   84
    Other Governmental Studies   85
    Descriptions of Proposals—Legislation   86
        Hawaii   86
        New Jersey   88
        The Hartke Bill   89
    Descriptions of Proposals—Governmental Studies   90
        Federal Role   90
        Maryland Planning and Zoning Law Study
          Commission   91
        Baltimore   93

Chapter	Page
Montgomery County, Maryland	93
Review of a Major Report	94
Douglas Commission	95
ACIR Report	98
Canadian Task Force Report	99
AIA Recommendations	99
Summary	100
Notes	101
11 SUMMARY AND CONCLUSIONS: ISSUES IN GENERAL LAND BANKING	104
Concept	106
Institutional Issues	106
Planning	106
Place in Government Structure	107
Powers	107
Political Concerns	108
Fiscal Impact and Equity	108
Land Market and Price Rise Effect	109
Operational Issues	109
Land Acquisition, Holding, and Disposition and the Decision Process	109
Scale of Operation—How Much Land?	110
Free Reserve	110
Eminent Domain	110
Sale Versus Lease	110
Legality of Land Banking	111
Financing	111
Evaluating the Operation	111
Note	111
APPENDIX QUESTIONNAIRE ON THE PUERTO RICO LAND-BANKING EXPERIENCE	
Relationship to Urban Planning	112
Purposes	112
Metropolitan Plan, Planning Process, Public Policies, and Land-Use Controls	112
Operations	114
Legal Factors	116
Financial Considerations	116
Structure	117

Chapter	Page
Overview—Conclusions	118
BIBLIOGRAPHY	119
ABOUT THE AUTHOR	124

LIST OF TABLES

Table		Page
1	Matrix of Land-Banking Concepts	4
2	Land Banking by Government Level	5
3	Compatibility of Land-Bank Goals	15

PART

I

**THE LAND-BANKING
CONCEPT**

CHAPTER 1

DEFINITION OF
LAND BANKING

The term "land banking" has been applied to a wide range of public and private activities in which land is held for future use. One writer has offered a matrix (see Table 1) that places in perspective certain types of public and private land-banking activities. It may be observed that certain private land-banking activities can be considered to supplement certain public land-banking activities where private land that is being withheld from development is consistent with the policies of such public land banks. One example of this is the holding from development of private land in the path of a planned development area under a general land-banking program.

This author has prepared a table (see Table 2) to put land-banking activities by various governmental levels in perspective (including the public activities listed in Table 1). All types of land-banking activities may be said to be intended to promote orderly development in one sense or another. However, it can be seen from Table 2 that the specific purposes to be served at different levels of government vary.

All public land-banking activities can be grouped into two broad categories—general land banking and project or special land banking. These terms have been used in Table 2 and are defined in the following paragraphs.

PROJECT LAND BANKING

Project land banking is first distinguished from general land banking insofar as it is concerned with a specific functional area. Activities that have been placed in this category include holding land for urban renewal, low-and moderate-income housing, open space, industrial development, and advance land acquisition for public facilities.

TABLE 1

Matrix of Land-Banking Concepts

Objectives	Structure (Model)	Operating Area; Size of Holdings	Capitalization	Relation to Private Real Estate Market	Relation to Public Planning
profit	large-scale builder community development corporation	limited and/or scattered	small	competitive; no effect on market	arm's length
profit	real estate investment trust	large-scale	large	competitive	arm's length
profit	new town developer	large-scale	very large	competitive on acquisition; control on disposition	private organization performs public functions
advance acquisition of sites for specific public purposes	housing development corporation land bank	limited	small	competitive; no effect on market price	preferential
advance acquisition of sites for wide range of public purposes	public development corporation	limited	medium	competitive	cooperative coordinated use of zoning permit, etc.
guide local or regional development	metropolitan development corporation	comprehensive	medium	competitive, though feed through to market price	department of local or regional government
control rate of land price inflation	public land authority	coterminous with metropolitan market area	very large	public monopoly; control	department of local or regional government

Source: Piedmont Triad Council of Governments, Land Bank Handbook, Advance Acquisition of Sites for Low and Moderate Income Housing (Greensboro, N.C., 1972). The views are those of the source and not necessarily those of this author.

TABLE 2

Land Banking by Government Level

Government Level	Primary Purposes	Land Bank Type[a]	Policy Framework
Federal	oversee federal lands	G	historical
Federal	possible involvement in land banking at all government levels in support of national policy	G, P	urban growth policy
State	environmental protection, new towns, large-scale public facilities	P	state planning
Metropolitan	control growth, land price; capture capital gains; land use; new towns[b]	G P	metropolitan planning
Local (single or multi-jurisdictional)	advance land acquisition for • public facilities • low- and moderate-income housing • industry • open space[c] • urban renewal[c]	P	 local planning local and metropolitan planning local planning local and metropolitan planning local planning.

[a]G—general land banking; P—project land banking.
[b]May or may not be within the context of general land banking.
[c]Technically not considered land-banking activities.

Source: Compiled by the author.

Other characteristics of project land banking that distinguish it from general land banking include the following: It is limited geographically to small areas; limited to individual jurisdictions; limited in size of land holdings; limited in level of impact on changing growth patterns, in influencing the land market, or in correcting an existing urban problem; and limited in time horizon, since it is aimed at relatively immediate implementation. Each of the functional categories presented here does not, of course, exhibit all of these characteristics.

A few examples will help clarify the meaning of project land banking. Urban renewal is concerned primarily with redevelopment of relatively small amounts of developed urban land in a single jurisdiction and is concerned with reducing the price of land through subsidy (write-down) in the project area. It has been argued that urban renewal does not constitute a land-banking activity, since it is desired that land be developed as soon as possible. In other words, urban renewal is not concerned with holding land for future use, or banking the land. (The fact that land under urban renewal often remains vacant for 10 or more years would not affect this argument—the distinction is, of course, academic.) Advance land acquisition for public facilities offers a similar example of project land banking. (It may be noted that advance acquisition is considered acquisition before the point in time after which not having the land will hold up the project. In many cases, however, acquisitions may occur quite far in advance of actual need.) Advance acquisition is generally concerned with specific small-scale public facilities (such as schools, parks, road right-of-way, etc.; advance acquisition may also apply to certain larger facilities of a "one-time" nature such as airports). It is intended primarily as a means of cost saving for municipalities, has little effect on controlling the private market, is generally a small-scale operation in terms of cost, and has little effect on controlling growth patterns. Certain programs, as well as individual purchases, can be held up as exceptions to these characteristics. One such exception is large-scale advance land-acquisition programs for highway rights-of-way, which can, of course, have a significant effect on desired growth patterns—if coordinated for this purpose.

To the extent that land banking implies the holding of land for future use, an argument may be made that open-space land acquisition is not a form of land banking. That is, the land is presumed to serve its intended use upon acquisition (unless some means of access, site improvements, etc. are needed) and is not intended to be reconverted to another use.

GENERAL LAND BANKING

This study is concerned with general land banking on a metropolitan scale. A comprehensive definition of general land banking in terms of purpose, scale, and method is as follows: the acquisition of developed and undeveloped land, holding of land, and disposition of land for all types of land uses—public and private—without prior specification of the use for particular sites, by a public body whose deliberate purposes are control of metropolitan growth pattern and/or regulation of metropolitan land prices and/or capturing of capital gains and/or regulation of land use.

The terms "acquisition," "holding," and "disposition" have certain implications that form a central part of the definition of general land banking. Acquisition can include acquiring land or interest therein by any and all means, including condemnation—"eminent domain." The use of eminent domain may be central to the operation of the general land bank. Holding of land is concerned with the policies of the land bank with respect to at least (1) the time frame needed for effectuating the objectives (possibly 20 or more years of land holdings); (2) the size of inventory presumed necessary to achieve the purposes; (3) the impact of land holding on the financing of the land bank; (4) site preparation, site assembly, project development, and provision of major infrastructure elements; and (5) management and interim use of the land. Land disposition may be by sale, lease, or other means and may entail certain conditions running with the land and/or project.

Policies with regard to land acquisition, holding, and disposition, such as use of strategic sites, have a major effect on the solvency of the land-bank operation, political acceptability, ability to achieve land-bank purposes, and similar considerations. These questions are discussed further in Chapter 7 of this book.

There are at present a number of land-banking activities for public and private uses, as noted earlier. A general land bank would not only be empowered to dispose of land for all purposes but would also not have to identify the purpose of specific sites at the time of acquisition. These characteristics raise a number of questions, including (1) which land to buy, when, and for what purposes and (2) which land to dispose of, when and for what purposes, to whom and at what price. These questions are also discussed further in Chapter 7. The use of eminent domain and the lack of specificity of future use of each site raise questions regarding the legality of general land banking, which are discussed in Chapter 4.

In order for a general land bank on the metropolitan scale to be effective, it may be assumed that some public entity at the metropolitan level must operate it. Except for areas with a general government encompassing the metropolitan area, there is no public entity now existing in U.S. metropolitan areas to carry out this function. Chapter 5 discusses this issue.

The definition just given includes two primary policies or purposes for general land banking: controlling metropolitan growth patterns and regulating metropolitan land prices. Other goals of general land banking have been identified to include the recapturing of gains to the public from public investment and the control of land uses through more detailed regulation. These purposes are discussed in Chapter 2. It is useful to note here that the two primary purposes are in conflict and will require a compromise in the operation of a general land bank. This is also discussed in Chapter 2. An overriding characteristic of a general land bank on the metropolitan scale is that it must operate throughout the metropolitan area on an "equitable" basis—that is, so that fiscal and other, similar major concerns of local governments are not disrupted as a result of land bank operation. If it does not, its policies will merely have the effect of redistributing growth and/or land values. The question of equity is discussed in Chapters 3 and 7.

The approach to general land banking on the metropolitan scale depends to a large extent on which goal—one of the two primary policies—controlling growth (growth strategy) and regulating land price (price strategy), or some other goal—is followed. The price strategy would alter our definition, in part, to read as follows: acquisition, holding, and disposition of land so as to regulate the general land price level. Under the price strategy, the acquisition program would be "haphazard." The growth strategy would alter the definition, in part, to read as follows: the acquisition, holding, and disposition of land in accordance with a comprehensive metropolitan plan. Under the growth strategy, land would be acquired in an "orderly pattern." The two strategies clearly imply certain differences, including the type of entity for operating the land bank (see Table 1) and different approaches to operation of the land bank.

The definition of general land banking does not necessarily imply a specific character of land to be acquired (developed or undeveloped), condition of structures thereon (blighted or unblighted), location of land within the metropolitan area (core, developing, or fringe area), or location of land to be disposed. Thus, in defining specific areas of operation of a general land bank, there must be a clear statement as to where in the metropolitan area land transactions can be carried out, what types of land can be acquired—namely, developed (both blighted and unblighted, the latter possibly being necessary to an overall plan, as often in the case of urban renewal) or undeveloped. It should be noted that such considerations make clear that a land bank is not necessarily operating to create an "immunizing belt of land around the metropolitan area" or to acquire land "in the path of development." To the extent of such specifications, the definition proposed earlier would be modified. Or, more to the point, the "definition" of land banking must be formulated on the basis of explicit consideration of the intent with respect to many of the factors mentioned, as well as others.

CHAPTER
2
GOALS OF
LAND BANKING

A number of purposes are expected to be served by governmental involvement in the land market in the form of land banking, including

1. shaping regional and community growth
2. curbing urban sprawl
3. capturing increases in land value created by governmental investment
4. improved management and control of the land market—also termed "perfecting the land market" and often viewed in terms of reducing land speculation
5. acquiring land for public uses
6. ensuring an adequate supply of land for certain kinds of private uses
7. protecting land with unique environmental qualities
8. lowering the costs of public improvements
9. lowering the costs of public services as a result of more compact development patterns
10. regulating the relationship among landowners
11. regulating land price
12. subsidizing low- and moderate-income housing.

These purposes are not independent in at least two respects. First, certain purposes are not compatible with others, and second, certain purposes may be either grouped or considered to be subsidiaries of broader purposes. Most of the purposes may be grouped under the heading Controlling the Urban Growth Pattern, with the remainder forming three distinct categories, as follows:[1]

A. Controlling the Urban Growth Pattern
    1. ensuring a supply of land for certain kinds of private uses
    2. ensuring a supply of land for certain kinds of public uses, including open space
    3. protecting land with unique environmental qualities
    4. decreasing cost of public facilities
    5. decreasing cost of public services as a result of more compact development patterns
    6. subsidizing low- and moderate-income housing

The rationale for this grouping is that embodied within the comprehensive planning process, wherein there is a set of social, economic, physical, environmental, and other goals that can be expressed more or less directly through the objectives listed. Curbing urban sprawl is not listed as an objective, since improving growth patterns presumes this to be one result. In addition, decreasing costs of public facilities and services is generally noted as a specific objective of curbing sprawl. The goal of controlling the urban growth pattern further assumes actions regarding the location, type, timing, and scale of development.

B. Regulating the Price of Land—improved management and control of the land market, also viewed as perfecting the land market and control of speculation.
C. Capturing Capital Gains—of increased value created by public investment.
D. Regulating Land Use—as an improvement over existing regulations.

While these are major goals, it should be noted that control of growth and regulation of land price are far more appropriate as underlying goals of a land bank program than capture of capital gains or regulation of land use. Further, other formulations of goals could result in a different approach than that presented in this chapter, particularly in the discussion of goal conflicts.

CONTROLLING THE URBAN GROWTH PATTERN

The meaning of orderly development may be expressed physically in terms of specific segments of a metropolitan area.

In a highly urbanized or developed area, usually called the core area, the basic concerns of physical development are with (1) redevelopment of extensive, blighted areas or of scattered sites; (2) development of scattered vacant sites; and (3) removal of nonconforming uses.

In a developing area—generally the area between the core and the fringes of the metropolitan area—orderly development is concerned with development of the land that has been "leapfrogged" or skipped over. The character of this part of the metropolitan area, generally termed "urban sprawl," has resulted in uneconomic extension of utilities and transportation facilities and higher costs of public services. A "social cost" of sprawl is the exclusion of low-income and minority groups due to the high cost of housing (as well as other causes, including exclusionary zoning).

At the fringe of the metropolitan area, where most future development is expected, the objective of orderly development is to attain the desired land-use patterns. The influence of sprawl has often resulted in characterization of development objectives for fringe areas as "avoiding urban sprawl."

Public involvement in the land market in terms of general land banking can play a role in each type of area. Within developed areas, urban renewal has attempted to perform the function of redevelopment. Land banking could include this function, as well as development or preparation for development of scattered vacant sites (including removal of nonconforming uses). Within the developing area, land banks could perform the same function with scattered sites.

At the fringe, the function of land banking would be more dynamic. It would be aimed at shaping the growth pattern of largely undeveloped areas and thus be used to assist in controlling the location, type, and timing of growth as well as "protecting" areas that public policy would not desire to be developed.

Existing experience and legal precedent in the United States is fully supportive of the second objective of controlling the urban growth pattern and is becoming more prevalent—at all levels of government, and particularly the state level—for the third objective. It is in the provision of land for certain private uses that the land bank must wrestle with an array of issues. As discussed in this study under "Existing U.S. Experience," land-banking activities currently exist for provision of land for industrial development and low- and moderate-income housing. However, in a general land-banking operation, all types of private land uses might be provided for. While it is presumed that comprehensive plans take into consideration social, economic, physical, environmental, equity, and other concerns, a land-bank operation must make all of these considerations, and others, sufficiently explicit so that decisions as to which sites to acquire and dispose of, when, to whom, and for what purposes can follow a rational and consistent line of reasoning.

The approach to controlling the urban growth pattern would involve the use of pricing policy as a regulatory mechanism. That is, when the purpose is to improve the direction of the location, type, and timing of land development according to land-bank policies, prices would be lowered in the strongest competition with the private market. Also, the amount of land prepared for development would be in close relationship to market demand. The overall thrust of the program might be to continually dispose of inward sites and acquire outward ones. This process is, of course, a simplified description of how the program might operate because of the type of activities in which it might be involved (extension, intension, development, redevelopment, etc.), the lack of fluidity of land availability, possible inability to react to the market, and so forth.

REGULATING LAND PRICE

Since land is one of the basic "factors of production," the benefits of reduced land price are quite evident. First, it would serve to directly reduce the cost of housing and other land uses, and second, reduced land price would also have a direct effect on lowering the cost of goods production.

One basis for having regulated land prices as a goal for a land bank is that speculative gain on land serves no social benefit except to those (speculators) who gain.[2] As indicated in the act establishing the Puerto Rico Land Administration (see "Existing U.S. Experience," Chapter 7), rising land prices cause problems in providing low- and moderate-income housing; they also make for undesirable urban expansion, creating financial burdens in the provision of public facilities and services, and increase the overhead costs of industrial and commercial enterprises, thus reducing their competitiveness. Moreover, rising land prices create large differences in individual incomes and prevent the implementation of the master plan.

At least three arguments have been identified for nonintervention in the land market by the "public".[3] These are as follows: (1) Should price effect be taken into consideration in making public decisions? (It is pointed out that public decisions, of course, have a differential effect on land price.) (2) Should the increased land value, due in large part to public investment, inure to the public? (Government decisions may have many secondary effects, and it may be unfair to single out land for retention of benefits to the public.) (3) Control of land price rise may have negative effects on the homebuilding industry.

It has been pointed out that regulating land price might be more directly achieved through direct price controls. It has also been observed that there are a number of means (at the federal level) for shifting the benefits among various interest groups (for example, tax policies, housing programs as levers in effecting land-use controls, assistance for public facilities, etc.).

The issues just raised are fundamental questions that cannot be addressed here. It can only be pointed out that many who have considered this question of public intervention to regulate land price (such as in the establishment of the Puerto Rico Land Administration, in the Douglas Commission's Recommendation No. 7b, and in other cases—see "Land-Banking Proposals," Chapter 10), have concluded that this is a warranted public function.

The approach to regulating land prices would have as its <u>end</u> the setting of land prices for land in a land bank, as opposed to the <u>setting</u> of land prices as the <u>means</u> for controlling growth patterns. That is, if the land bank disposes of land at the "going price structure," then it acts simply as another, albeit large-scale, competitor. Prices must therefore be set in competition with the market to have the effect of regulating land prices in the private market.

In order to affect the private market, under either a "growth" or a "price" strategy, the land bank must have a "free reserve" sufficient to sustain competition. This reserve would consist of land ready for urban use by the private market (that is, excluding land committed for public facilities, under lease, and not prepared for immediate use). The need for such a reserve holds very significant implications regarding the administration of the land bank program—namely, the types of activities that it undertakes and how, and the time necessary to acquire and prepare sufficient reserves. One source has noted in looking at foreign experience that "of all the municipal land reserves considered, only . . . that of Oslo, Norway . . . seem(s) extensive enough and free enough to be a useful bulwark against any substantial speculation. But in the more usual case, if the incentives for speculation are strong, then a city that fights speculation with palpably insufficient reserves is only forcing the speculators to hold on a while longer. It does not change their expectations, but only forces them to wait a bit, and it may not even do that."[4]

CAPTURING CAPITAL GAINS

The basic argument for the capture of capital gains by the public is that the rise in land values is largely attributed to public investments. The capture of such gains would be accomplished by periodically raising land rents (for land uses for which the program leases rather than sells the land). One problem with this process is the conflict between the land bank's desire to capture such gains and the lessee's desire for security.

REGULATING THE USE OF LAND

Regulating land use is, to a large degree, closely associated with the goal of controlling the urban growth pattern. The approach to such regulation would be through the attachment of restrictive covenants on land sales and conditions in leases. It is possible to be more detailed through this approach than through general ordinances.

GOAL CONFLICTS

Some of the main goals of general land banking are in conflict and would require at the minimum a trade-off between the goals and the operation of the program and at the maximum a clear delineation as to what the goals of the program are to be. The following paragraphs discuss goal conflicts and compatibilities among the four goals discussed earlier. Table 3 schematically shows these conflicts and

TABLE 3

Compatibility of Land-Bank Goals

	Goal		
	Regulate Land Price	Capture Capital Gains	Regulate Land Use
Regulate growth pattern	(-)[a]	(+)[b]	(-)
Regulate land price		(-)	(-)
Capture capital gains			(+)

[a] Minus sign (-) indicates general incompatibility between goal in vertical column and horizontal row.

[b] Plus sign (+) indicates general compatibility between goal in vertical column and horizontal row.

Source: Compiled by the author.

compatibilities. The minus sign (-) indicates that the goals in the vertical column and horizontal row are not compatible (for example, Regulate Growth Patterns and Regulate Land Price are not compatible goals). The plus sign (+) indicates the reverse.

With regard to the goals of controlling the growth pattern and regulating land prices, there are at least two basic conflicts. The first deals with acquisition-disposition policy. In an effort to control land price inflation, the land bank would acquire tracts offering the largest ratio of future value to present price. By virtue of this process, land would be acquired haphazardly without regard to existing land-use plans. (The more "valuable" sites may not be the most desirable for orderly development.) Since land was not acquired with regard to the master plan, it is likely that the land disposition program would not be consistent with the plan[5] and might, in effect, create a "counterplan."

The second conflict concerns pricing policy. As noted earlier, under a growth strategy prices would be set in relation to desired pace of development. Under a policy of regulating land prices, it would always be desirable to sell far below the market rate.[6] (It should be noted that the setting of prices presumes a sizable free reserve.)

To some extent, regulation of land use is also in conflict with growth control. That is, where land-use regulations—sale covenants or lease conditions—are too strict, they would put the land bank at a disadvantage relative to the private market. The goals of growth control and capturing capital gains appear to be compatible.

To a degree, the goals of regulating land prices and capturing capital gains are in conflict, since lower land prices result in lower rents and thus lower "gains." This may not, however, represent a serious conflict. Regulation of land use conflicts with regulation of land price for the same reason that it conflicts with growth control.[7] Finally, the goals of regulating land use and capturing capital gains appear to be compatible.[8]

SUMMARY

Two primary goals have been identified for general land banking on a metropolitan scale: controlling the urban growth pattern and regulating land price. Other goals are capturing capital gains and regulating land use. The meaning of orderly development depends in part on the segment of the metropolitan area in which the land bank is active; however, general land banking is concerned essentially with guiding the location, timing, and type of development in the metropolitan area. This goal raises an array of policy questions needed to clearly define "orderly development."

The values to be gained in regulating land price are based on the social disbenefits and economic implications of speculation. Capturing gains to the public resulting from public investments is also seen as a justifiable public policy. Whether this is the proper role of government, and whether land banking is the proper mechanism for achieving this goal, are open questions.

The two primary goals of general land banking have been shown to be in conflict, as are certain of the other goals. This will require trade-offs between the goals and the actual operation of the land bank.

This review of the purposes and approaches to general land banking and the goal conflicts involved raises questions on the theory, practice, and practicality of general land banking. Some of these questions may not be capable of answer through research. Others may be approached in terms of means of overcoming or moderating the expected effect.

NOTES

1. Urban Land Research Analysts Corp., Municipal Land Reserves Policy: An Analytical Study of Foreign Experience (Lexington, Mass., 1968), pp. 121-140.
2. Charles M. Harr, Wanted: Two Federal Levers for Urban Land Use—Land Banks and Urbank (U.S. Congress, House, Committee on Banking and Currency, June 1971), p. 935.
3. Sylvan Kamm, Land Availability for Housing and Urban Growth (U.S. Congress, House, Committee on Banking and Currency, June 1971), pp. 271-272.
4. Urban Land Research Analysts Corp., op. cit., p. 129.
5. Sylvan Kamm, Land Banking: Public Policy Alternatives and Dilemmas (Washington, D.C.: The Urban Institute, 1970), p. 13.
6. Urban Land Research Analysts Corp., op. cit., p. 140.
7. Ibid.
8. Ibid., p. 138.

CHAPTER 3
RELATION TO PLAN IMPLEMENTATION

The effectiveness of a land-banking program in assisting plan implementation will depend, to a large extent, on the characteristics of the planning process, the physical plan, and other land-use controls. The land bank will also have effects on the process and form of physical plans. This chapter attempts, first, to describe the present state and problems of plan implementation in the United States, and second, to identify specific improvements in plan implementation that are considered necessary, by some, without land banking and that may be prerequisite to a metropolitan land-bank program.

PLANNING AND PLAN IMPLEMENTATION

The objectives to be obtained by any given community may fall into a number of broad categories, including size (population, acreage, housing and other facilities, etc.); shape; level of economic activity (as measured by income characteristics, community economic base, etc.); quality of life (physical beauty of natural and man-made features, social life and composition of the community, health, safety, etc.); equity (distribution of income and social goods); and economic efficiency (provision of public facilities and services at minimum costs). The last category includes efficiency of transactions in terms of land transactions, or "perfection of the land market".[1]

A variety of means—social, economic, physical, political—in coordination are required to accomplish a community's objectives. Such objectives may relate in a variety of ways to a comprehensive land-use plan. To the extent that a community's objectives are clearly expressed, to the extent of their expression in the comprehensive plan, and to the extent that such plans are carried out, comprehensive planning can provide a contribution to accomplishing community desires.

In 1967, John Reps, a noted authority on city planning in the United States, eloquently summed up the plight of plan implementation in noting that land-use patterns in American cities have not reflected the plans of local governments and have resulted in an urban environment that is " . . , inefficient, inconvenient, unattractive, uneconomical, and unloved. . . ."[2] In effect, land-use plans are not implemented —to our detriment. Reps described what he considered to be three basic approaches to city planning in this country. These are (1) long-range master planning (regarding which he noted, as have others, that the techniques available are not effective in carrying out the plan), (2) locating communities and employment centers with the expectation that desired land-development patterns will follow, and (3) a method he called "disjointed incrementalism," which seeks to solve problems in order to provide improvement over the present.[3]

It is not our purpose to debate the virtues or problems associated with these methods. It is to point out, however, that general land banking (1) certainly cannot be carried out in the context of the third approach, (2) must be aided by the second approach, and (3) must be viewed in the context of an improved approach to long-range planning.

A report prepared by the American Society of Planning Officials (ASPO) entitled Metropolitan Planning Policy Implementation has taken a disciplined view of present approaches to plan implementation in the United States. The intent of that report was not to identify new means of plan implementation but rather to identify a process for metropolitan agencies to examine questions of implementation. The main conclusion of that report is that ". . . such agencies are not devoting systematic attention to developing the implementation components of their programs."[4] The report reviews the basic strategies currently used for plan implementation (including providing advice and information, encouraging cooperation and coordination, and ad hoc problem solving, among others) and stresses that plan and policy development must be shaped by available implementation techniques.

In 1969, a report was prepared by the Metropolitan Washington Council of Governments (COG) entitled The Changing Region. Its purpose was to provide a comparison of plans and policies for the Wedges (relatively open areas) and Corridors (relatively developed areas) Plan with development trends during the 1960s. The general conclusion of this report was that plans and policies differed significantly from development trends.[5]

The report identified basic problems with plan implementation and also noted areas of significant progress. The latter included retention of open space; acceptance by area jurisdictions of the planned-community zoning concept; adoption of zoning ordinances to allow a variety of housing types; adoption of fair-housing ordinances; adoption of certain highway and transit plans that will help the plan; and public incentives through planning and tax benefits to promote private renewal and redevelopment. It can be observed from this list that in no case (except the last) have public policies been devised to enforce the plan.

In contrast to the areas of progress, the COG report identified "major shortcomings in obtaining regional development policies." Some of these are as follows: insufficient and scattered open space; improperly planned sewage facilities; little use of low-density zoning to implement the wedge concept; insufficient low- and moderate-income housing and little impact on housing needs provided through urban renewal; inadequate timing in highway and transit plans to support the plan; limited value of planned transit facilities in implementing development on the urban fringe; equal highway access to both wedges and corridors; and unexpected population growth. The report also noted uncomplementary local and regional policies, regional policies in conflict (such as increased public facility availability raising housing costs), and vagueness of certain policies (such as town centers—it is unclear as to how local policies, federal employment policies, and private development will be coordinated). It also mentioned another problem: inadequate analytical tools for determining whether the area is obtaining its objectives.

This array of problems is certainly not characteristic only of the Washington metropolitan area. It does point up in a graphic way, however, some of the hard questions that must be faced if metropolitan planning is to be effective. The report concluded that "new ways to implement development objectives must be found . . . plans must be prepared which are more realistic . . . and, better techniques must be devised to measure the impacts of growth, and to measure the impact of policy decisions."[6]

LAND-USE CONTROL

Grace Milgram has classified land-use controls in terms of their "level of interference with the private market." These are (1) provision of information, (2) extension of public facilities, (3) zoning and subdivision regulations, (4) manipulation of land taxes to induce or inhibit development, and (5) public acquisition of land and/or rights therein.[7]

As seen in this typology, land acquisition is the most "radical" of the possible means of public intervention. Where such acquisition is to serve the needs of providing sites for certain public uses, there is little disagreement as to its validity. The current study views such public intervention in general land banking as being more than this. The following pages present some thoughts on the needs for improvements in each of the categories noted previously, as well as in planning and governmental structure.

Provision of Information

One area in which the planning profession has been highly active has been in the field of providing and evaluating large masses of data in diverse areas dealing with population, employment, housing, economic conditions, and transportation, to name a few. With regard to land development, it is noted, however, that little is known about the land market, and in particular no usable information exists about the value and characteristics of land transactions.

Extension of Public Facilities

Control over public improvements—their location, type, and timing—has been identified in all quarters of the planning field as a vital need for directing growth. This is concerned with such facilities as major highways and water and sewer lines, and with capital improvement programs for other public facilities. Mention is seldom made of controlling utilities for directing development (probably because these are more or less privately provided), although they too can be of influence—as prime movers rather than as followers of development. More recently, and particularly in the Washington metropolitan area, the availability of sewer capacity has been recognized as the basis for limiting the location and timing of development. This concept has been further broadened to encompass the available capacity of other public facilities such as schools and public services as necessary prerequisites to properly timed development of certain types.[8] Taking this concept a step further, it is noted that proper pricing of public facilities can also influence development. Such pricing is aimed at seeing that new development at the fringes pay their "fair share" for the extension of public facilities. It is argued that since those in highly developed areas and those at the fringe of development pay the same rate for use of public facilities, those in the closer-in areas, in effect, subsidize facility extensions.

Zoning and Subdivision Regulations

Among land-use controls, zoning is the single most-used technique. It is defined as the regulation of land use under the police

power, without compensation, to promote health, safety, morals, and welfare. Zoning has been criticized as being ineffective in controlling urban growth, as a static, prohibitive control and one that cannot change quickly enough with changing community goals. Specific criticisms of zoning include the following:
1. It cannot account for market forces.
2. It is too inflexible where new land-use types are developed.
3. It cannot remove nonconforming uses.
4. It is weakened by spot zoning and variances.
5. It is inflexible in terms of the time required to change the zoning ordinance.
6. It is difficult to administer, requiring the obtaining of many consents.
7. It has been used for negative purposes such as segregating economic, social, and racial groups.
8. It designates zones in vacant areas with no basis in fact for the "proper or likely future land use."
9. It cannot encourage desired land uses.[9]

Numerous attempts have been made to identify means for correcting these "deficiencies." Some means are through improvement of zoning as currently constituted, others through new zoning techniques, and yet others through the courts, as with restrictive zoning based on racial considerations. Recommended changes in zoning have included planned unit development, floating zones, conditional zoning, and compensatory payments, among others.[10] While it is accepted theory, in planning, that zoning be based on a comprehensive plan, in practice this too needs to be fully recognized as a needed improvement in zoning. The broader recommendation concerned with the administration of zoning is that there be more direct involvement by levels of government higher than the local jurisdiction or that responsibility for zoning be shifted to a higher level of government such as the state.

Major drawbacks cited against subdivision regulations as a land-use control are (1) that inflexible standards are applied to all land-use types, regardless of the peculiar circumstances of development (it should be noted that development approaches such as planned unit development, large-scale shopping centers, and industrial parks tend to counter this criticism), and (2) that they often require developers to dedicate—unreasonably—portions of their sites for public services (this approach has, however, been cited as one reason why advance land acquisition for public facilities may not be a major necessity for more common public facilities such as schools and smaller parks).

Manipulation of Land Taxes

Land taxation has a significant effect on the type, timing, and location of development. The basic change called for in tax laws from the viewpoint of planning is the need for having higher assessed rates and capital gains taxes to reduce land holding for speculation in order to encourage desired forms of development. An American Institute of Architects (AIA) task force has stated these problems in terms of removal of tax disincentives that are impediments to building and rebuilding at a neighborhood level, need for tax incentives, and need for property tax reforms to reduce distortion of local markets.

One authority on suburban land conversion (Allan Schmid, author of Converting Land From Rural to Urban Uses)[11] believes that a major explanation for lack of implementation of land-use plans is that the competition to capture land value appreciation in terms of expectation of the use of parcels for high-valued uses (such as shopping centers) of necessity creates pressure against maintenance of the plan. On this basis Schmid concludes that market forces must be shaped in the same direction as broad public policy.

With this basic direction, Schmid identifies means by which the gains resulting from speculation can be reduced—that is, captured by the public while not inhibiting the land conversion process. The basic thrust is either to increase capital gains taxes on changes in land use by rezonings; through public purchase for the purpose of land assembly and preparation for quick resale, as by development districts, which would also reduce or eliminate speculative gain based on the degree of density of the proposed use; or through development easements, which would purchase the development rights of the landowner by paying the difference between present and estimated future value of the planned use. In summary, there are clearly a variety of methods that might be tried for directing market forces along public policy lines. Schmid feels that " . . . equity in sharing of future gains will be a key ingredient . . . "[12] in instituting new patterns of population settlement. That is, as long as some property owners will be able to achieve future gains, others will not be willing to "give up their chances," even if they are compensated for existing land value. Schmid thus concludes that a combination of the methods described here, centered on public "capture" of a large part of the land-value change, will be needed in order to better direct the urban development pattern.

PLANNING IMPROVEMENTS

A number of the recommended changes noted earlier could certainly fall into the category of planning improvements. To these can be added the following list: sharpening of economic analyses and identification of costs and benefits (and to whom they accrue)—and more important, working with a variety of public interest groups as well as the political process; a minimum scale of development that might be specified for certain parts of metropolitan areas; restructuring of categorical grant programs; increasing the quantity of new housing; and opening the suburbs to low- and moderate-income housing.

IMPROVEMENTS IN GOVERNMENTAL STRUCTURE

While improvements in the planning process and land-use controls are necessary, they are not necessarily sufficient for implementing land-use plans. Diverse sources have called for the restructuring of the governmental process for directing development. Such recommendations generally call for improvements of planning at all governmental levels, as well as new forms of government, and have been embodied in bills on urban growth policy, as described in this study for the Hartke bill and the Humphrey bill ("A Proposal for Achieving Balanced National Growth and Development").

These recommendations would encompass entities such as national agencies for administering national policy for urban development, more effective state planning agencies and state development authorities (New York State's Urban Development Corporation being cited most often), regional planning and development agencies, and metropolitan planning and development agencies. It has also been suggested that government reorganization should consider abolishing the smaller units of local government, developing metropolitan government, and sharing revenues and costs on a metropolitan basis.

The report cited earlier (Metropolitan Planning Policy Implementation) listed a number of other institutional changes for metropolitan planning agencies (MPAs), including (1) obtaining, where not already available, or strengthening mandatory referral powers so that denial by the MPA means something; (2) greater financial independence of the MPA by obtaining nonearmarked state funds or imposing tax levies; (3) removing certain land-use control powers from local governments and placing them within the MPA; (4) obtaining power to either directly or indirectly plan and operate certain regional facilities and systems, and the power to raise taxes to maintain them; and (5) combining several regionwide special-purpose authorities and the MPA into a metropolitan development government.[13]

In an effort to gain further insights into relationships of metropolitan land banking to metropolitan plan implementation, an interview was held with Krishna Murthy, assistant director of regional planning at the Metropolitan Washington Council of Governments. Mr. Murthy was in agreement with certain of the needed planning improvements noted earlier and also identified specific needs in land-banking strategy, in capital improvement programing, and in zoning

With regard to strategy he suggested that the land bank prepare development plans for certain periods such as 5, 10, 20, and 30 years. This would begin to address the acquisition, holding, and disposition decision-making process concerning which land to acquire and dispose of, when, and for what purposes. Another part of the strategy would deal with scale of development. Murthy noted as an example the AIA recommendation of developing neighborhood-size units as being appropriate for a metropolitan land bank. Also stressed was the need for an evaluation process for jurisdictional fiscal impact by the program. One major problem facing the land bank cited by Murthy (and Clawson) was the lack of sufficient data on the land market. He further noted that the availability of data such as land value projections would itself influence the development process.

As currently practiced, capital improvement programs (CIPs) are prepared for 5- to 6-year periods. Murthy noted that the concept of a mid-range (for example, 15-year) CIP would be strongly supportive of, and probably necessary for, mid-range strategies of the land bank. Difficulties noted with the mid-range CIP included the need for early political decisions and assurance of financing.

One zoning policy that was suggested as supportive of land-banking strategy is that of large-scale development units noted earlier. This holds specific implications with regard to the use of sale or leasing in land disposition, as well as the general ability to manage the land bank program. As a general commentary on land banking, Murthy suggested that it may be more practical to institute a number of jurisdictional land banks within a metropolitan area in the contexts of, among others, metropolitan planning, metropolitan equity, and metropolitan-level policy decisions in "critical areas" such as water supply and the CIP.

SUMMARY

The general relationship of public intervention in the land market—or land banking—to improvements in planning, plan implementation, land-use controls, and governmental and institutional structures can best be summed up in a presentation of the conclusions on these subjects of a number of authorities in the field of urban planning.

Many of the needed changes in planning, plan implementation, and land-use controls cited earlier were made by Marion Clawson and Anthony Downs. From the perspective of both planning experts, all of these changes (those that they individually recommended) taken together will not be sufficient to direct metropolitan development. Comments by Clawson (an authority on suburban land conversion) were included in the areas of planning, zoning, research, and timing and location of public improvements and assessment of their cost (pricing); in suburban land conversion regarding land-marketing information, changes in tax laws, and reducing land speculation; and with regard to abolition of small-unit government, establishment of metropolitan government, and institution of shared metropolitan costs and revenues. In light of these recommended changes, Clawson concludes as follows:

> Measures to make the present suburban land conversion process work better, to improve the functioning of the urban land market, and to reorganize local government might well have considerable importance. But, could they be sufficient without public acquisition of land, even under the best of circumstances? In the judgement of this writer, they could not. If we wish really to cure the major deficiency in the suburban land conversion process, public land purchase must be initiated and carried out on an adequate scale.[14]

Downs' recommendations were in the areas of planning, zoning, and governmental structure for effective planning. In the same vein as Clawson, Downs concludes as follows:

> Any attempt to exert significant public influence over the nature, location, magnitude or physical form of urban growth requires public ownership or other direct control of a significant part of the land in a major metropolitan area, especially on the growth periphery. Leaving most of the control over land use in private hands, especially where private ownership is fragmented due to thousands of small parcels, as in the U.S., makes it impossible to impose any real guidelines for development policy on even one metropolitan area. This conclusion implies that creation of an overall "urban growth strategy" or "urban land policy" would involve radical restructuring of traditional land ownership and control arrangements in the

U.S. Also, development of any significant number of nonmetropolitan new cities, or even peripheral or satellite cities, will require public ownership of much of the land in those cities.[15]

Two recent statements by the AIA task force further point up the position of public intervention in the land market with respect to land-use controls and planning effectiveness. Regarding land-use controls, the task force states that: "There is no one specific mechanism for controlling and arresting urban growth and rebuilding, but the principle of public determination of where such development takes place is essential."[16]

With respect to the perspective on urban planning, the task force concludes that

> finally, we are convinced that any effective national growth policy requires that land development increasingly be brought under public control. This is true particularly of land which lies in the path of growth or that otherwise is crucial to the community's well-being—open space, flood plains, coast and shores, etc.
>
> We favor public acquisition and preparation of land in advance of development. We believe that the appreciating value of urbanizing land should be recycled into the costs of developing, serving and maintaining it. We believe that in many cases, leasing rather than outright sale would be desirable for land acquired and assembled by public action.[17]

Similar conclusions regarding land-use controls were reached in the enactment of the Puerto Rico Land Administration Act in 1962, where it was stated that

> this ever increasing price of land cannot be controlled nor the problems thereby created can be solved, by any of the tools available to the Commonwealth and municipal governments; that the levy of taxes and the regulation of physical planning are insufficient; the regulation on zoning and subdivision operates prospectively for undeveloped and underdeveloped areas and cannot prevent the undesirable, but legal, use of the land; and that the regulation of land subdivision is insufficient to control either the expansion of city limits or the disconnected and inadequate expansion of the cities.[18]

From the descriptions just given it is clear that much can and should be done short of public intervention in the land market. There is, of course, no guarantee that all the improvements, taken together, will be sufficient to implement metropolitan plans. Certain problems of plan implementation may be "solved" by public land banking. However, public land banking alone—without other changes—cannot be expected to implement metropolitan plans.

NOTES

1. Urban Land Research Analysts Corp., Toward More Efficient Programs of Land Use Controls (Lexington, Mass., 1969), p. 8.
2. John W. Reps, "The Future of American Planning—Requiem or Renascence?" Land Use Controls 1, no. 2 (1967): 1. It should also be noted that in this article Reps presents many of the basic arguments for land banking.
3. Ibid., pp. 2-3.
4. American Society of Planning Officials (hereafter, ASPO), Metropolitan Planning Policy Implementation, Planning Advisory Service (hereafter, PAS) Report no. 262 (Chicago, Ill., October 1970), p. 1.
5. Metropolitan Washington Council of Governments, The Changing Region (Washington, D.C., 1969), pp. 48-49.
6. Ibid., p. 49.
7. Grace Milgram, The City Expands (Philadelphia: University of Pennsylvania, 1967), pp. 132-133.
8. Labarbara Bowman, "Montgomery Acts to Cut Growth," Washington Post, June 27, 1973, pp. C1, C8.
9. Urban Land Research Analysts Corp., Municipal Land Banks: Land Reserve Policy for Urban Development (Lexington, Mass., 1969), pp. 21-25, and American Institute of Architects (hereafter, AIA), A Plan for Urban Growth: Report of the National Policy Task Force (Washington, D.C., 1972), pp. 5-6.
10. David Heeter, Toward a More Effective Land Use Guidance System PAS Report no. 250 (Chicago, Ill.: ASPO, 1969), pp. 12-15.
11. Allan A. Schmid, "Suburban Land Appreciation and Public Policy," Journal of the American Institute of Planners (hereafter, JAIP) 36, no. 1 (January 1970): 38-43.
12. Ibid., p. 43.
13. ASPO, op. cit., p. 17.
14. Marion Clawson, Suburban Land Conversion in the United States: An Economic and Governmental Process (Baltimore, Md.: The Johns Hopkins Press, 1971), p. 355.

15. Anthony Downs, "Alternative Forms of Future Urban Growth in the United States," JAIP 36, no. 1 (January 1970): 7.
16. AIA, op. cit., p. 11.
17. Ibid., p. 4.
18. Richard P. Fishman and Robert D. Gross, "Note, Public Land Banking: A New Praxis for Urban Growth" (23 Case W. Res. Law Rev. 897, 1972), p. 20.

CHAPTER

4

**LEGALITY OF
LAND BANKING**

The major issue involved in the legality of general land banking is whether the public taking of land for unspecified use—on the basis of promoting orderly development—will be upheld by the courts. Some researchers who have looked specifically at the case material related to this question have concluded that it would in fact be upheld. In a recent note on the subject, the American Law Institute cited cases pro and con but did not take a position in either direction.[1]

In terms of whether general land banking can be attempted in the United States, its legality is, of course, of first importance. Considering that such legality cannot be clearly shown at present, there is little that can be added on the subject in this study. In this light, the following discussion is presented in order to document the basic thinking on this subject by those who have examined it.

SELECTED LEGAL OPINIONS

In a study sponsored by the U.S. Department of Housing and Urban Development, it was concluded that "our research into Constitutional and Statute Law in the United States suggests that no fundamental legal difficulty stands in the way of establishing such land banks or endowing them with the powers needed for carrying out their principal tasks."[2] In discussing this subject, the authors start with the premise that regulation is not sufficient for adequate planning. The most basic municipal planning powers are zoning (under the police power) and eminent domain. The power of eminent domain (to condemn land) is limited by use of the land for public purposes and awarding the holder just compensation. The authors note that a broad interpretation of public purpose has opened the way for improved land-use control through compensated acquisition. They state further that there is flexibility in ownership which can never be matched by any regulatory scheme for controlling land use.

The potential for governmental control through ownership is evident in the fact that municipalities could use the same methods of dividing land as private owners, including dividing the land in "time" and ·pace (horizontally and vertically), in ownership and use (easements, covenants), and through rights of sale or lease with conditions.

The powers of local governments are those granted explicitly by the state and the implied powers necessary to carry out those expressed. Municipal corporations have both governmental powers (promoting the general welfare) and proprietary (providing public works and operating revenue-producing powers facilities). According to the study, "there seems at present to be no explicit provision about land reserve policies."[3] Specifically, the authors note that no statutes appear to expressly authorize the capture of capital gains or the control of speculation as objectives of a land reserve policy. However, a policy incorporating these purposes "would probably not be invalid."[4] On the other hand, purposes of land-reserve policies that do generally fall within municipal authority include "better planning, control over urban development and redevelopment, and the adequate provision of public facilities."[5] The latter are generally expressed in most city-planning acts based on the Standard City Planning Act (U.S. Department of Commerce, 1928), which calls for the broad plan objectives of ". . . guiding and accomplishing a coordinated, adjusted, and harmonious development of the municipality. . . ."[6] While it is accepted that a municipality has the power to plan for the land it owns, the major question facing the land-reserve policy is whether a municipality can acquire and dispose of land for this purpose. It is noted that all but one state requires enabling legislation for urban renewal, in which case land acquisition depends on evidence of blight in a designated urban renewal project. Thus, it is not clear whether these statutes would suffice to enable a land-reserve policy. Over and above the question of acquisition, additional laws would be necessary to establish that the method of operating the land reserve is reasonable.

A similar opinion on this subject was offered from another source as follows:

> The governing principles . . . are the same under most of the State Constitutions as they are under the Federal Constitution. If the goals of the government project are beneficial to the community and the use of condemned property bears a reasonable relationship to these goals, then the public use requirement is not a bar to condemnation. And possibly more important, a legislative

determination of the appropriateness of condemnation is accorded a very strong presumption of validity. In few modern cases has a court found that public use was not what the legislature had determined it to be. Although prompting orderly growth differs in some ways from slum rehabilitation, slum prevention and the like, it is extremely unlikely that a court that has sanctioned these latter programs would hold, contrary to a legislative determination, that curbing urban sprawl and maintaining rational growth were not a public purpose.[7]

As described elsewhere in this study, a land-banking agency—the Puerto Rico Land Administration (PRLA)—was established in 1962, representing the only case found by this author of a large-scale, multipurpose land-banking operation in the United States. The act establishing the PRLA gave it authorization to acquire land through condemnation (as well as other means) to hold for an indefinite period (except in the case of land for public facilities, in which case the period is 15 years) to fulfill land-banking activities. In a case testing the ability of this authorization—Commonwealth v. Rosso—it was upheld by the Supreme Court of Puerto Rico ". . . in a unanimous and exhaustive opinion. . . ."[8] An attempt was made to bring the case into the United States Supreme Court, which dismissed the appeal ". . . on the ground that the case failed to present a substantial federal question."[9] Thus, it was concluded that ". . . presumably then, the Supreme Court of the United States is in full agreement with the high court of Puerto Rico: land banking—while not factually identical to other examples of eminent domain cases that have received the sanction of the courts—falls easily within existing constitutional principles that have been established to regulate governmental takings."[10] It is noted, however, that the individual states would have to approve this concept under their own constitutions, and legislation would be likely to do so.

One final note can be added from a report by the Advisory Commission on Intergovernmental Relations, which reviewed the subject in terms of land acquisition for new towns and stated the following:

> The exercise of land purchase and eminent domain powers could face legal barriers in some states. Yet, it is already clearly accepted in virtually all the states that where land acquisition through purchase or eminent domain involves clearing of blighted land for subsequent sale to private developers, it is a public use and a permissible exercise of public authority. Moreover, it is

also accepted in nearly all the states and in federal urban renewal legislation that public acquisition may also include . . . land which is predominantly open and which, because of obsolete planning, diversity of ownership, deterioration of structures, or site improvements, or otherwise, substantially impairs or arrests sound growth of the community.[11]

These legal precedents in urban renewal provide a basis for a policy that asserts that planned urban development of vacant land to avoid subsequent blight and deterioration is as justified a public objective as the removal of blight and deterioration after it has occurred.[12]

EMINENT DOMAIN

It is generally felt that the power of eminent domain is necessary for an effective land-banking program. A number of issues are associated with the use of this power, including (1) the problem of court cases; (2) the possibility of a high court award, which may result in high land prices for other parcels; (3) political problems, which may result in adverse public reactions to the taking of private land with the fear of arbitrariness. However, it may also be pointed out that having the power may itself make negotiations easier, especially when an owner does not wish to go to court or would gain if the land were condemned rather than simply sold.

NOTES

1. The American Law Institute, A Model Land Development Code, tenative draft no.5 (Philadelphia, Pa., March 1973), pp. 55-60.
2. Urban Land Research Analysts Corp., Municipal Land Banks: Land Reserve Policy for Urban Development (Lexington, Mass., October 1969), p. 235.
3. Ibid., p. 150.
4. Ibid., p. 151.
5. Ibid.
6. Ibid., p. 152.
7. Richard P. Fishman and Robert D. Gross, "Note, Public Land Banking: A New Praxis for Urban Growth" (23 Case W. Res. Law Rev. 897, 1972), pp. 956-957.
8. Ibid., p. 959.
9. Ibid., p. 961.

10. Ibid.
11. Advisory Commission on Intergovernmental Relations, Urban and Rural America: Policies for Future Growth (Washington, D.C., 1968), p. 162.
12. Ibid.

This book was prepared prior to the availability of the American Law Institute's tentative draft No. 6 of Article 6, Land Banking (dated April 15, 1974).

Tentative draft No. 6 goes into detail on the organization, policy, and powers of a land bank agency, land acquisition, management and disposition policies, taxation of the agency and its property, condemnation, and local government role.

CHAPTER 5

STRUCTURE FOR LAND BANKING

GOVERNMENTAL LEVELS

Determination of the appropriate type of entity for administering a general land bank on a metropolitan scale must flow from a set of assumptions about the purposes to be achieved and the ability of the entity to carry these out in terms of legal, financial, political, and planning consideration, among others. Clearly, growth is a metropolitan phenomenon, and metropolitan planning must be keyed to local and metropolitan concerns. To some extent land markets are also metropolitan in nature. Among the existing forms of government that might take on the land-banking responsibility are the federal government, state governments, metropolitan governments (where existing), councils of governments (COGs—which are not actually governments), and local jurisdictions. (In a report prepared for the U.S. Department of Housing and Urban Development entitled <u>Municipal Land Bank: Land Reserve Policy for Urban Development</u> by the Urban Land Research Analysts Corporation, the question of "who should administer the metropolitan land bank is left open with alternatives offered an overall metropolitan authority, where it exists or can be brought into successful existence . . . to the state . . . to the federal government for control or coordination. . . .")[1]

Federal

Charles Harr has presented the reasoning for federal involvement in establishing land banking and recommends formation of metropolitan governments rather than federal activities in metropolitan land banking. This rationale deals with (1) the federal responsibilities to ensure that federal funds are properly used and (2) ensuring that federal policies (such as those dealing with population distribution, housing, environment, poverty, etc.) are carried out.

State

Harr has also pointed out certain responsibilities reserved to the states in controlling the land that make state involvement in metropolitan land banking indispensable. These include settlement of disputes over land in state courts (laws dealing with common-law nuisances, contracts, and leases); state constitutions detailing land-use regulations (building codes, zoning, subdivision regulations, official maps, street controls, etc.); taking of land for public purposes (eminent domain); and property and land taxation.

A number of pros and cons have been identified regarding a state-level agency concerned with metropolitan land banking. Advantages include easier sources of financing and an overview of metropolitan and state development and regulatory powers, as noted earlier. Disadvantages could include dependence on annual appropriations and political insensitivity to metropolitan needs. That is, such an entity would be politically responsible, but not directly to those most immediately affected—namely, the residents of each metropolitan area. There is also a strong argument that a state-level entity is not able to determine the best interest of each metropolitan area.

Metropolitan

At present there are only a few metropolitan governments in the United States, and these do not have broad development powers. Clearly, a metropolitan government would be the most desirable entity for administering a metropolitan land bank from the standpoint of political accountability and metropolitan planning and objectives. As noted previously, such an entity would probably require state authorization for land banking and may, of course, be dependent on state and federal financing.

Councils of government are noted here for the purpose of identifying all possible land-bank entities. While these organizations are composed of elected officials from area jurisdictions, they do not have development responsibility. Operation of the land bank by a council of government would have to rely on cooperation, which is not a reasonable basis for administering such an operation.

Local Jurisdictions

Administration of a metropolitan land bank by a central city or other individual local jurisdiction in a metropolitan area would not be feasible because of legal constraints on its ability to acquire land in other jurisdictions (even considering extraterritoriality for acquiring land for certain public needs). Such individual jurisdictions are also inappropriate as metropolitan land-bank entities in terms of metropolitan planning and objectives and political accountability.

In essence, then, there is no existing entity (except for localities with metropolitan governments) that might properly take on the responsibility of metropolitan land banking. In the Hartke bill on urban growth policy, metropolitan development and planning agencies are proposed. Development agencies might be a proper vehicle for metropolitan land banking if they have political responsibility and are closely tied to the metropolitan planning agency. Another entity that has been cited as appropriate for operation of a metropolitan land bank is a public corporation, a concept that is discussed in the following paragraphs.

PUBLIC CORPORATIONS

Portions of this discussion of the desirability of a public corporation for administering a metropolitan land bank are taken from an article entitled "Note, Public Land Banking: A New Praxis for Urban Growth,"[2] which concludes, after reviewing alternative methods for administration of a land bank, that the only logical land-bank agency is a public corporation. Such a corporation has been used in the past for water and sewer districts and other general purposes.

Special-purpose public corporations have been defined as corporate bodies authorized by legislative action to function outside of the regular structure of state or local governments in order to finance, construct, and usually to operate revenue producing enterprises. Advantages of a public corporation include the following:
1. It is better able to meet metropolitan problems.
2. It can secure its own revenues without full faith and credit of the state.
3. It is outside constitutional limits of state and local debts.
4. All revenues are its own, as opposed to being divided among state agencies.
5. It provides ease of management regarding legal, financial, and personnel needs.
6. It is relatively autonomous, having no direct voting constituencies, and therefore is relatively nonpartisan.

7. Overlapping terms of directors ensure smoother operations.
8. It is tax exempt on bonds and real estate.

Sylvan Kamm has noted that it is possible for a public corporation to be structured so as to be politically accountable. The structure of the corporation could include heads of local governments, heads of state agencies, and local planning officials, among others.

Jurisdictional approval might be general in approving an overall plan or specific in review of each land transaction in the respective jurisdictions. While the corporation might thus be politically accountable, it might be, as Kamm states, "cumbersome and time consuming." This may suggest the need for means to overcome objections of individual jurisdictions to decisions that would promote the general welfare.[3]

OTHER STRUCTURAL APPROACHES

This study, and particularly this chapter, has approached the concept of developing land banking on a metropolitan scale in terms of a fully constituted metropolitan entity dealing with the entire metropolitan area and concerned with all land-use types.

Two other approaches have been identified by the author for establishing metropolitan land banking. One approach would involve the aggregation of general land banks of jurisdictions in the metropolitan area. The other would involve the aggregation of metropolitan-level project land banks. Detailed consideration of these approaches is not within the scope of this study. A few comments will be made here, however, concerning the pros and cons of these approaches.

Aggregation of General Land Banks

The essence of this approach is that all major jurisdictions in the metropolitan area would create general land banks that would somehow be coordinated in the framework of metropolitan planning and policies. One virtue of such an approach is that it is more practical from technical and political standpoints to create jurisdictional as compared to metropolitan general land banks because of the nature of the issues that would face each approach. A central question facing such an approach is whether it is possible to coordinate (interpreted broadly) such individual operations in a metropolitan framework. Many other issues can quickly be identified with this structural approach.

Aggregation of Project Land Banks

There are project land banks in the United States for industrial, housing, public facilities, and open space. Urban renewal encompasses other private uses as well. If such project land banks were created in series, at the metropolitan level, and under a single entity, this might be more politically feasible than creating a full-scale general land bank on a metropolitan scale and might also provide a framework for learning how to administer (interpreted broadly) general land banking. Clearly many difficulties would face such an approach, including types of issues associated with general land banking as discussed in this study. In terms of the development of this structural approach, a central issue is how the changing goals would be balanced as additional land-use functions are added to the structure.

While these two approaches entail many difficulties, each deserves further investigation to determine whether each might be feasible in whole or in part.

SUMMARY

The central issue arising from this chapter is clearly that of whether metropolitan land banking is feasible in the absence of metropolitan government.

At present almost no metropolitan area in the United States has an existing entity that could take on the responsibilities for general land banking on the metropolitan scale. Entities at the federal, state, and local government levels suffer most from lack of direct political accountability to those affected—metropolitan area residents—and are not sensitive to metropolitan needs and planning. Councils of government do not have needed legal responsibility for administration of a land bank. While metropolitan government is most desirable, few exist. Under the present structure of government, without creation of metropolitan governments, it would appear that a public corporation would be the best alternative for administration of a metropolitan land bank. Such corporations have many advantages but may also prove ineffective in carrying out metropolitan purposes without, among other things, reasonable mechanisms for overcoming the objections of local jurisdictions. Such corporations will present particular difficulties in metropolitan areas that include parts of two or more states, since different laws, regulations, and the like will affect the land-banking entity.

The preceeding discussion has not touched upon specific relationships between a metropolitan land-bank entity and a metropolitan planning agency (MPA). This is one of the most critical questions in the effectiveness of a land-banking program in metropolitan plan implementation. Questions like the following must be addressed in this area: (1) Would the land bank be a subsidiary of an MPA carrying out the plan under its guidance, or would it be a separate entity interpreting metropolitan plans as it develops strategies? (2) As a separate entity, what legal relationships would exist with the MPA to ensure that the land-bank policies conform to the plan? (3) A number of improvements in the planning process, plan implementation, land-use controls and governmental and institutional changes are discussed in this study. Possible powers and/or responsibilities for land-bank types of entities have been recommended in recent proposals. Which of these are appropriate for the MPA and for the land bank? These questions and others must be part of the process of defining what a land-bank agency is and can do in the planning process.

Two other structural approaches to developing a general land-banking operation on a metropolitan scale were identified. These are aggregation of jurisdictional general land banks in a metropolitan framework and aggregation of metropolitan-level project land banks. Each deserves further investigation as to their feasibility.

NOTES

1. Urban Land Research Analysts Corp., Municipal Land Banks: Land Reserve Policy for Urban Development (Lexington, Mass., October 1969), p. 196.

2. Richard P. Fishman and Robert D. Gross, "Note, Public Land Banking: A New Praxis for Urban Growth" (23 Case W. Res. Law Rev. 897, 1972), pp. 942-945.

3. Sylvan Kamm, Land Banking: Public Policy Alternatives and Dilemmas (Washington, D.C.: The Urban Institute, 1970), pp. 26-27.

CHAPTER

6

FINANCING

Numerous problems are associated with financing a large-scale land-bank operation. Some of these are availability of sufficient funds during the initial start-up phase, when little or no revenue (except possibly from interim-use rents) will be coming in; the need to balance land-bank objectives with financial objectives; the need for large-scale funding sources; and the need for continuing funding availability. This chapter concentrates on approaches to funding.

It must be recognized that the financing of a land bank depends on many factors such as scale of operation; metropolitan area size; goals; land-bank structure; legal limitations; acquisition, holding, and disposition strategies, and the like. In short, the financial feasibility of land banking is at once a most complex issue, one of the most important to political decision makers, and one needing intensive consideration of alternative approaches.

As a public corporation,[1] two methods might be used to finance a land bank. These are (1) government funds in the form of grants or loans and (2) debt financing through issuance of its own securities. With regard to government financing it can be noted that local governments generally do not have sufficient funds to meet existing expenses. The more likely sources of government financing, so far as fund availability is concerned, are the state and federal governments. Both state and federal governments have long supported programs associated with urban development that include land acquisition and site preparation (such as urban renewal, water, sewer, and transportation programs, open space, new communities, industrial development, and advance land acquisition for public facilities). These programs might be used directly to jointly finance a land bank, or separate appropriations might be made for land banking on a noncategorical use basis. The latter would be preferable in terms of continued funding availability and the ability to implement land-bank goals.

In the start-up phase, grants or long-term, low-interest loans would be needed when financing is by government, local, state, or federal.

As a public corporation, there are a number of factors that favor debt financing by a land-bank agency. These are (1) exemption from federal income taxes on interest, thus lowering borrowing costs; (2) exemption from federal income taxes on revenues; and (3) possible exemption from local real estate taxes. The latter, of course, may present problems for local governments and may therefore require payments in lieu of taxes or some other method to permit the sharing of appreciated land value. In contrast to the advantages, it has been noted that at start-up the land-bank operation may have difficulties in marketing its bonds due to lack of taxing powers and financial history. One approach to overcoming this problem is that used by the New York Housing Finance Agency and Urban Development Corporation: A capital reserve fund has been established into which go all funds from the state, revenue from sale of securities, as well as revenue from other sources. Sufficient funds must always be in the reserve to cover the following year's cost of principal and interest. If sufficient funds are not available for these costs, the New York State Legislature is committed to appropriating the difference, in this way providing a guarantee of a sort for the agency's security holders.[2]

As reported elsewhere in this study, Charles Harr has proposed metropolitan land banking and has also proposed a federal urban development bank—as Harr terms it, "Urbank."[3] The purpose of the Urbank would be primarily to provide loans to state and local governments for capital facilities. It would be organized as an instrument of state and local governments but with Presidentially appointed directors. Federal guarantees would be provided on its bonds, and loans would be made to state and local governments at below market interest rates "even given tax exemptions."

Harr neither recommends a method for financing metropolitan land banks nor links the Urbank to it as a financing tool. With the sizable funding required for a metropolitan land bank, and with the need to "spread the risk" of such an undertaking, the Urbank proposal, along with other revenue sources (such as land-bank bonds, land-bank tax revenues, interim-use rents, and grants), would appear to be worthy of long-range consideration. Since the Urbank does not exist, however, it is necessary for an initial metropolitan land-bank program to devise financing means that are readily attainable.

To gain insight into the financial aspect of land banking, an interview was held with Patrick Noonan, president of the Nature Conservancy.[4] This organization is "devoted to the preservation of ecological and environmentally significant land." It reports the conservation of nearly 380,000 acres of such land since its first acquisition in 1954.

In recognizing the complexity of the concept and practice of metropolitan land banking, Mr. Noonan was quick to note that many factors must be considered in devising a financing scheme. One primary factor noted was the size of the metropolitan area in which land banks should operate. This would dictate, among other things, the amount of land needed by the land bank, land costs, and thus the level of financing. Clearly, the smaller the area, the more manageable would be the operation as well as the financing.

Another major point made by Noonan was the desirability of private involvement in the land bank, not only in terms of development of land but also as a source of financing. It should be noted that the Nature Conservancy depends on contributions from the public, grants from foundations, and membership dues. Noonan suggested consideration of the financing of a land bank by such sources as insurance and underwriting companies and banks with an agreed-upon fixed-percent profit. He further suggested that this be the limit of "control" over the land bank on the part of such sources.

Considering the importance of the need both for practical means of financing and for large amounts of funds, the author would agree that such private financing sources should be investigated. However, it will be noted that this study has viewed the land bank as a public operation in terms not only of structure but also of the goals to be achieved and the exercise of significant powers. In this light, it is necessary that particular attention be given to (1) how control of the land bank by private financing sources would be limited and (2) what mechanisms would be established to ensure the fixed-percent profit suggested by Noonan.

Finally, it should be noted that Noonan left open for consideration other revenue sources such as bonds, grants, loans, general tax funds, and use of capital gains taxes.

As mentioned earlier, a question facing the land bank is the balance between financial and land-bank objectives. If, for example, objectives include low- and moderate-income housing requiring a write-down, or provision of land uses such as open space or public facilities that might "pay less" for available land sites than some private uses, the land bank must balance these objectives against a higher price for, or return on, its land, which would, of course, help "balance" the books. Clearly, this type of situation must arise if the land bank is to fulfill public policies rather than private development objectives. While certain conditions may be placed on the agency, such as a maximum percentage of write-down or portion of holdings devoted to public uses, this nevertheless will be a serious and continuing issue.

Regarding the problem of the need for a continual source of funds, Sylvan Kamm has identified at least three possible sources of revenue for the land bank that would operate like a trust fund. These would include transfer fees on real estate transactions, allocation of capital gains taxes in connection with land transactions, and allocation of increments in property taxes resulting from increased assessments in land values. He aptly notes for the latter source of funds that this presumes a rapid and accurate reflection of higher land estate values. This source of funds, of course presumes that higher land taxes will be an acceptable result of metropolitan land banking.[5]

Certain other considerations may also moderate the financial problems of land banking. For a land bank that operates under a full lease policy, payments for land for public facilities will still be in full, since such land would be sold rather than leased. There are less-than-fee methods for acquiring land that should reduce the immediate financial impact on the land bank. As indicated in the law establishing the Puerto Rico Land Administration,[6] prices of land to be acquired by the land-bank agency may be "frozen" so as not to reflect the activity of, or the announcement of the intent to acquire by, the land bank. Finally, as suggested by Herbert Bab, the land bank may be given the sole right for rezoning, which would encourage early land sales to the land bank at lower prices.[7] Another technique that would encourage early sales to the land bank would be that proposed in a bill introduced in the New Jersey State Legislature that would have a landowner wait two years for the land bank to make a decision as to whether or not to purchase the site.

NOTES

1. This discussion is based in large part on Richard P. Fishman and Robert D. Gross, "Note, Public Land Banking: A New Praxis for Urban Growth" (23 Case W. Res. Law Rev. 897, 1972), and Sylvan Kamm, <u>Land Banking: Public Policy Alternatives and Dilemmas</u> (Washington, D.C.: The Urban Institute, 1970).

2. Fishman and Gross, op. cit., pp. 968-970.

3. U.S. Congress, House, Committee on Banking and Currency, Subcommittee on Housing Panels, papers, Charles K. Harr, <u>Wanted: Two Federal Levers for Urban Land Use—Land Banks and Urbank</u>, June 1971, p. 942.

4. Interview with Patrick Noonan, President, The Nature Conservancy, August 13, 1973.

5. Kamm, op. cit., p. 32.

6. Fishman and Gross, op. cit., p. 922.

7. Herbert J. G. Bab, "New Policies to Control Land Use in Hawaii" (unpublished draft), chap. 3, p. 1.

CHAPTER

7

LAND ACQUISITION, HOLDING, AND DISPOSITION

MARKET FRAMEWORK

Development of a land bank is often described in terms of two basic phases. These are, first, the "gearing-up" phase, during which land is inventoried by the land bank, and second, the operational phase, during which the land bank would have a significant influence on the land market in terms of influencing prices and/or growth.

It must be said that this may not be a correct model of the way the land bank would operate. The factors that influence the entire land-conversion process, land-bank goals, and practical considerations of producing a "result" would very likely require the land bank to operate dynamically—that is, in a continual process of acquisition and disposition beginning soon after start-up.

In any event, unless it is presumed that the land bank would immediately be empowered—and funded—to acquire all the land necessary for its purposes—a highly unlikely situation—it must be presumed that the decision-making processes for the land bank for acquisition holding, and disposition of land in carrying out its objectives must be made within the context of the ongoing land market.

The land bank must be concerned with land markets in all parts of the metropolitan area—developed core, developing area (often termed the area of urban sprawl), and conversion at the fringe—and possibly beyond the fringe, including the relation to adjacent metropolitan areas as well as understanding of national trends. It must also differentiate between demand for raw land and for improved sites. The land bank must be aware of "consumer" demand for housing and other land uses; be knowledgeable in the decision processes of landowners, land dealers (or speculators), and land developers; and know the "prices" at which land is sold. Marion Clawson has noted with respect to the latter that "although purchases and sale of suburban land are an extremely important aspect of land use in the United States today, very little dependable information is available about them."[1] He has also stated that very little is known about the actual operation of land markets and the decision processes of various "actors."

However, it is just this understanding that is necessary in determining if land banking is feasible or desirable, in devising the land bank's decision processes, and in evaluation of the land bank's effectiveness.

From the foregoing, it is clear that the subject of the relation between the land bank and land markets is well beyond the scope of this study. The purposes of this chapter are therefore to discuss some of the major operational issues in land banking; the decision processes for acquisition, holding, and disposition of land; and certain specific issues in the latter areas.

MAJOR OPERATIONAL ISSUES

How Much Land?

In answer to the question of how much land is required by a land bank to carry out either of its main goals in growth control or reducing land price rise, Sylvan Kamm could only offer the conclusion "just as little as possible in order to achieve its objectives."[2] He notes that "there would be immense variations depending on the strategies employed, it would vary from area to area depending on physical and economic characteristics and the dynamics of the growth process, and would probably have significant variations over time."[3] While attempts certainly can and must be made to answer this question at the outset, the land bank will probably not know how much land it needs until it "gets there." Clawson has said that "as a first approximation, one may suggest that the agency should seek to have 60 percent or more of the land in the general area within which it operates, and that it should seek to acquire lands for more than five years ahead, generally for more than ten years ahead, and often up to twenty years ahead."[4,5] This percentage would allow the land bank to have a major role in suburban land development yet leave a significant private land market. This would also help avoid some of the disadvantages Clawson sees of ownership of all undeveloped metropolitan land by a land bank, such as the errors resulting from lack of competition and the need to accept all development applications in the absence of competition (or prepare an adequate defense for nonacceptance).

Land Price Rise

As noted earlier, the land bank is conceptualized as going through two stages—gearing up and fully operational. It has been pointed out that, under either a price or a growth strategy, during the gearing up phase the price of land bought by the land bank would rise and the price of land not bought would also rise. Clawson notes that the degree of price rise of land-bank land would depend on "the amount of land purchased, timing of acquisition relative to the suburban land conversion process, the pace of acquisition and the urgency with which the land bank agency moved to bid up and acquire land as well as other factors."[6] With regard to the rise in price of land not bought by the land bank, he notes that the price rise would be due to "lessened supply and higher value expectations." He also notes that within a metropolitan area land values in a portion of the area where there is little land banking might go down, since little growth might be expected in that area; but on the whole the effect of land banking would be to raise the price of privately held land.

While Clawson concludes that the price of land acquired would probably rise, he states that ". . . in actuality we do not know . . ."[7] what the effect would be or how much. This is, of course, a significant question and may only be answerable once a land bank is in operation—and perhaps not even then. It is another concern in a continuing evaluation of the effects and effectiveness of the land bank. All of this depends on the elasticity of supply and demand for undeveloped suburban land (and redeveloping land), which indicates the policy significance of estimating these elasticities.[8]

Regarding this price rise phenomenon, Sylvan Kamm rhetorically raises the question, "but wouldn't this be only a temporary effect which would be more than offset when the land bank reached an operational status in which it was disposing of land at a rate at least equal to that at which it was acquiring it?"[9] As with the questions of how much land is needed for control and what would be the price effects, he answers by stating that "this is not at all clear because the bank would itself be caught up in the inflationary spiral it has generated."[10] That is, the land bank would continually be paying higher prices for each new parcel acquired, which would result in either higher disposition prices or the need for subsidies. If subsidies are required, the question must be asked as to whether the same objectives could be better accomplished through other forms of subsidy. This is one of the central questions of the desirability and feasibility of metropolitan land banking.

Land Taxes

Land taxation has been mentioned in another part of this study as one form of land-use control that can be effectively used in plan implementation. In the context of land banking, taxation policies are not merely a supportive factor in carrying out the land-bank objectives but rather an integral factor in land-banking feasibility and the effects of public intervention in the land market.

There are two separate but related questions that must be addressed concerning land taxation. These deal with tax revenue from land not bought by the land bank and tax payments on land that is bought. With regard to the first question, Clawson has observed that if the value of land not bought increases, the additional tax revenues thus generated would help "pay" for the land-bank program. This, of course, supposes that the higher value and possibly higher assessment will be socially, economically, and politically acceptable. Other sources of revenue might include interim-use rents and special tax revenues. With regard to the issue of tax payments by the land bank, it might be assumed that taxes or payments in lieu of taxes (since public entities normally do not pay taxes) will be made. If not, the total burden will fall on all other landowners.

As with other issues raised earlier, it is not necessarily clear as to what the impact on land taxation would be.

Equity

Land-bank holdings would inevitably be concentrated in specific jurisdictions under a price or growth strategy, thus affecting such jurisdictions most. However, if a land bank is to operate on a metropolitan scale, there must be metropolitan equity. This suggests the need for redistribution of tax burdens among the jurisdictions. It also must lead therefore to redistribution of metropolitan land values as well as equality in distribution among jurisdictions of land-bank financing and revenues.

The foregoing clearly leads to the need for assessing the fiscal picture of all jurisdictions in a region and the devising of a process of equitability that is dynamic—that is, requiring constant scrutiny. Many other factors would need to be considered in determining the impact of tax policies. One would be the point at which the total tax increases on unbought land and taxes on land-bank land represent a significant fiscal impact. This question could depend on the total size of land-bank holdings, land-banking strategies, the effects of other land-use controls, cost savings, and the like. In other words, this, too, would be part of the continuing evaluation process.

In discussing the impact of fiscal disparity and criteria for evaluating tax treatment one source has noted that

> ... discussions of highway siting, airport location, and industrial zoning are rarely restricted to the merits of the alternatives from the perspective of the best pattern of development for the region as a whole, but instead such decisions become politicized by efforts of local groups to attract property which will generate local fiscal gains. The correlation between taxes paid and services received is now dependent on the luck that one has in getting wealthy neighbors. A reduction in this dependence on the wealth of one's neighbors, in order to get "good" tax treatment, will increase the likelihood that development decisions will be made on more "rational" grounds—the real costs of providing services and the real net advantages of development.[11]

A criterion of "location neutrality" (location neutrality says that the tax price—tax per unit of public service—should be the same for a given individual no matter which neighbors he chooses to live among nor which neighbors choose to live near him) is offered that, if achieved,

> ... would remove one of the false signals (tax advantage) guiding individual locational decisions and would thus lead to a more satisfactory development pattern in the Metropolitan Area. Consideration of the best use of land would take precedence over the land's best use for fiscal goals. Achieving locational neutrality would also remove a major incentive to fiscal zoning and competitive behavior of local governments which inhibits cooperative development of the Area.[12]

It is within such a context that a land bank must consider the metropolitan equity of its policies and operations.

The preceding discussion shows that there are complex relationships between, on the one hand, at least the following: land-bank strategies regarding acquisition, holding, and disposition of land; total land holdings at any given time; pace of acquisition; and land ownership concentrations; and, on the other hand, at least the following: metropolitan physical and economic characteristics; land supply and demand elasticities; price rise of land-bank and private land; the effect of the inflationary cycle; and taxation. These and other factors must be considered, then, in making the decision to attempt to enter land banking. They will also be of continuing importance in guiding the land bank and evaluating its effectiveness.

LAND BANK DECISION PROCESS

The land bank must have a clearly defined process for decisions on land acquisition, holding, and disposition. Basic questions of acquisition include which parcels to acquire, when, by what means, at what price, and for what purposes. (As noted in the definition in Chapter 2, one characteristic of general land banking is the ability to take land without specifying its future use. This does not remove the need to consider future use in decision making.) Holding or management policy is concerned primarily with interim use. Questions of disposition include which land to dispose of, how, when, to whom, for what purposes, and at what price.

To assist in the decision-making process, cost-benefit relationships based on monetary factors can be envisioned encompassing the acquisition, holding, and disposition of land. One author has looked at this subject, although the approach is admittedly not extensive or rigorous.[13] According to the model proposed, economic costs would include acquisition cost, land holding or interest cost, management and improvement cost, and acquisition and disposition transaction costs. Financial benefits include interim-use rents. Taxes are not considered a cost, as explained in the discussion elsewhere in this chapter. Other considerations in such a cost-benefit framework are also discussed under land disposition in this chapter. The author of this model explained how linear programing and heuristic (rule-of-thumb) modeling might be applied and showed how complex a problem this is in terms of only financial considerations.

The decision process must also consider a myriad of factors directly and indirectly associated with the land bank, such as (1) indirect costs and benefits; (2) interdependence among parcels; (3) acquisition, holding, and disposition methods; (4) market dynamics; (5) the land bank's total financial situation; (6) policies and changes outside of the direct influence of the land bank; (7) political impact; and so on. Some of these are discussed elsewhere in this chapter. It is sufficient to note that the decision process calls for extensive data on the direction of growth, land transactions, price patterns, and the like; modeling techniques; and a carefully defined framework for consideration of all pertinent factors. A continual process would be necessary to assess the implications of decision-making and land-banking effectiveness.

METHODS OF ACQUISITION

Considerations in how to acquire land, as noted by Kamn, include negotiated purchase versus condemnation, use of fee or less-than-fee acquisition, and methods of payment.[14]

With regard to condemnation, it was noted in the discussion of land-banking legality that this has certain inherent problems such as length of time, court proceedings, political liability, and the price effect on future acquisitions. To say the least, it is desirable not to use condemnation except where necessary. A number of methods may be used for acquisition, including fee, development rights, easements, acquisitions subject to life estate, and lease-back, to name a few. However, "while any land banking proposal must consider the potentials of less-than-fee acquisitions, they are still only potentials whose usefulness still remains to be proven in the types of situation which would be encountered in acquiring control in an urbanizing setting."[15]

Methods of acquisition payment might include cash, installment purchase, and credit purchase. For the land bank, a cash purchase would be advantageous during a tight money market but would require commitments of the total land price and payment of carrying charges on this amount. For the land seller, cash payment may result in higher capital gains taxes (unless the land is taken through condemnation). Installment purchases would benefit the land bank in terms of more fluidity of funds and in negotiation, and the seller in terms of capital gains taxation. Credit purchases through use of the land bank's credit instruments may have certain benefits if they are tax exempt. The effectiveness of this method would depend in part on the confidence of the market in the land-bank securities.

Kamm has pointed out some considerations in acquisition associated with price and growth strategies. For the price strategy, he boils acquisition policy down to a process of "obtaining the best bargains," which requires sensitivity to the direction of growth, pricing patterns, and special opportunities. The major problem cited is the possibility of obtaining the wrong parcel.

A number of considerations were listed earlier for decision making. Certain problems are associated with some of these factors. Acquisition in accordance with the comprehensive plan makes the process "more difficult and costly because it causes the land bank to operate in a restricted market (that defined by the plan) with all its cards on the table."[16] While in certain countries, such as Sweden, secrecy is used to avoid this result, this approach is questionable in terms of the long-term process unless all acquisitions remain secret until disposition (and perhaps not even then). That is, even if private landowners are not immediately aware of the land bank's holdings,

51

the eventual disclosure will begin to show certain trends. This problem is clearly evident when private developers acquire land for new towns. In the case of Columbia, Maryland, the announcement of the intent to create a new town was made only after nearly all the land had been acquired in order to avoid the price rise and holdout by landowners. Kamm has also suggested that guidance by the plan will result in forcing the land bank into greater use of eminent domain, especially as key parcels become necessary for fulfilling the objectives.

Two very basic questions for planning in the United States must also be considered. One is that the planning process is not geared to identify land-bank needs (that is, when and where and for what purposes land should be used). The second consideration is the continuing viability of the plan and commitments of public facilities. Kamm comments that "to achieve this might requires isolation of the land bank, the planning agency and the public works financing process further from the political process than is either feasible or desirable."[17]

These considerations raise basic issues about the planning processes practiced in the U.S. Land banking is an active rather than a passive force like other land-use controls (except for taxation, which is not widely used for plan implementation). It is not sufficient to picture land banking in the context of the present planning process, not only because of the problems noted earlier but, more important, because public ownership of the land will have the effect of changing the process. It may, for example, make the concept of new towns more viable within a metropolitan area, since this is a definable entity for land-bank operation. It will also "force" more explicit public decision on subjects such as location of low- and moderate-income housing and programing of public facilities.

Present planning relies on assessment of historical changes, estimates of future changes, and hoped-for influences of public decisions on private decisions. Land banking will attempt to act dynamically to fulfill expectations through its policies and strategies and will therefore be a relatively "known" quantity in influencing change.

LAND HOLDING OR MANAGEMENT

From the viewpoint of land-bank operation, there is only one specific question with respect to land holding or management—that is, interim-use policies. One other subject may also be noted here for convenience—that is, land-bank functions regarding land assembly, subdivision, and improvement.

Two broad categories of interim-use policies can be identified. For land that is already in agricultural or urban use, the land bank may have a lease-back policy in order to gain revenues. For vacant land, developers may wish to erect a structure such as small-scale roadside services. The land bank must therefore be able to define interim uses and their duration. A relatively short amortization period may be one criterion. The implications of allowing construction of any kind should be explored, since even "interim use" may begin to influence the future land-use pattern.

Policies with regard to land assembly, subdivision, and site preparation will have to be defined in light of many factors noted earlier, especially the physical goals of the comprehensive plan, marketing strategies, and the desirability of the land bank's having the function of project administrator and/or developer.

DISPOSITION

The central issues of land disposition are these: (1) What use is to be made of the land? (2) What should be the disposition price? (3) When should land be disposed of? Policies must also be developed regarding sale, lease (and other disposal means), and development controls.

The question of what use is to be made of the land may be viewed from a number of perspectives, as follows:

1. Methods for deciding among competing uses. Assuming that within the general plan (as within most zoning categories) more than one land use is appropriate for any particular site, this may suggest an "auctioning" policy by the land bank to determine the "highest and best use" and, of course, obtain the maximum "price" of the land.

2. Associated with item (1) is the question of determining when specific land-use types should be permitted. An example of this is the desire by private developers to erect a shopping center not far from another center. The land bank must either address the issue of whether it gets involved in "competition" or follows only a policy such as is noted in item (1).

3. Subsidy of certain land uses. The most often cited example for subsidy of land use is the provision of low- and moderate-income housing. The land bank must have explicit policies on this matter, since the subsidy of one use is at the expense of others and affects the land bank's financial situation. One possible approach that has been suggested is the setting of a maximum percentage of disposed land (or of some other unit or combination of factors) in a given period such as a fiscal year. One minor problem with this is the lack of knowledge of total land disposition for the year until the period has elapsed.

4. Associated with item (3) is the need for policies regarding disposition of land for private and public uses, with the latter assumed to pay a lower price for the land. The effect of land disposition at a price lower than can be obtained can be viewed as a form of subsidy. To some extent, the land-banking process should be expected to incorporate a process for prior identification of land needs for public uses. However, as conditions change, specific situations can be expected in which such decisions will be required. An example would be competition between open space and industrial development. An even more extreme example would be competion between low-income housing and industrial use (since the low-income housing already requires a subsidy).

These questions, in effect, begin to form the basis for policies regarding the location, type, timing, and scale of development that are the central purposes under the growth control strategy. Clearly these are only part of the larger question of controlling the rate of metropolitan growth, as discussed in the chapter on land-bank goals.

Sale Versus Lease

There are pros and cons to both the buyer and seller under sale or lease policies: ". . . to the extent that financial concerns are critical to a land bank, the best probable solution is to authorize the use of both methods."[18] Restrictive covenants or deed restrictions may be conditioned with sale or lease. However, the lease may make such restrictions more easily enforceable by giving the land bank continued control, especially at the time of lease renegotiation. Leasing also has the appeal of making a later renewal or redevelopment easier, since the land remains under land-bank control. With regard to lease renegotiation, a process must be established and tied to factors such as market conditions, price indexes, and the like. Kamm has noted that a lease arrangement may result in poor property maintenance toward the end of the lease period, since there is no incentive for upkeep. Means would have to be devised to deal with this problem. In the Canadian Task Force report (discussed elsewhere in this study), it was suggested that leasing might be limited to nonresidential and large-scale developments.

It has also been noted that a lease policy may result in political difficulties—that is, pressures to keep rents low (particularly in election years).[19] Solutions recommended include tying of rents to official price indexes; adjudication based on price indexes, land market, needs of the parties, and social convenience; periodic auction of leaseholds or freeholds as yardsticks (noted to be a difficult process); and penalty fees against the land bank, in which the lessee must give up the premises if rents are set too high. It was noted that widespread leaseholds in Israel and Great Britain are considered an "infringement on personal liberty" and that leaseholds are not traditional in the United States.[20] Another source notes that ". . . record keeping for a large number of leased properties is no small responsibility and requires considerable expense to perform satisfactorily. There also can be speculation and profiteering in leased land to illegal subleases unless careful control is maintained. If the intent is to retain the full gains for the state, such factors can be detrimental."[21]

Development Controls

A range of development controls might be considered by a land bank, including architectural criteria, subdivision and zoning characteristics, minimum time within which development must take place, and sublease or resale conditions (to avoid speculation among other considerations). A process of controls review must also be devised. Too strict regulations might have the effect of raising prices. This fact should influence the "level" of control relative to the private market.

Disposition Price

As noted earlier, a cost-benefit evaluation can be established to assist in determining disposition prices. Also, the issues raised previously concerning the use to which land will be put will have a strong bearing on disposition price. Nevertheless, it is reasonable to aim at a disposition price that will cover costs, including acquisition, net holding (where there are interim rents), administration, site preparation, and subsidy (to cover subsidized uses and open space, the latter being non-revenue-producing). The disposition price might also include a markup if the price calculated on this basis is less than that based on market appraisal, although this would be questionable in light of the goal of reducing land prices.

NOTES

1. Marion Clawson, Suburban Land Conversion in the United States: An Economic and Governmental Process. (Baltimore, Md.: The Johns Hopkins Press, 1971), p. 350.
2. Sylvan Kamm, Land Banking: Public Policy Alternatives and Dilemmas (Washington, D.C.: The Urban Institute, 1970), p. 39.

3. Ibid.
4. Clawson, op. cit., p. 359.
5. It may be noted that certain foreign countries have land reserves for up to 20 years of growth needs (see Chapter 9, "Foreign Experience").
6. Clawson, op. cit., p. 137.
7. Ibid., p. 138.
8. Ibid.
9. Kamm, op. cit., p. 39.
10. Ibid., p. 40.
11. Metropolitan Council of the Twin Cities Area, The Impact of Fiscal Disparity on Metropolitan Municipalities and School Districts (Saint Paul, Minn., March 1971), p. 17.
12. Ibid.
13. Urban Land Research Analysts Corp., Investment Policy for Land Banks (Lexington, Mass., 1967), p. 1.
14. Kamm, op. cit., pp. 33-38.
15. Ibid., p. 37.
16. Ibid., p. 41.
17. Ibid.
18. Ibid., p. 49.
19. Urban Land Research Analysts Corp., Municipal Land Reserves Policy: An Analytical Study of Foreign Experience (Lexington, Mass., 1968), P. 133.
20. Ibid., pp. 133-135.
21. Center for Urban Development Research, Public Land Acquisition for New Communities and the Control of Urban Growth: Alternative Strategies (Ithaca, N.Y.: Cornell University, March 1973), p. 37.

PART II
HISTORICAL BACKGROUND

INTRODUCTION

There are a number of activities within the United States (including Puerto Rico) that have been termed land banking or are closely related to the land-bank concept. In many other countries, public and semipublic ownership of large amounts of land has been found to play a central role in the course of urban development. Chapters 8, 9, and 10 present a review of land-banking experience in the United States, including proposals for land-banking operations, and land banking in other countries.

The basic purposes of this review are, first, to establish the general validity of the land-bank concept as a means of carrying out public policies and, second, to identify the implications of available experience for metropolitan land banking within the United States. Emphasis is placed on land banking as a concept, since there are clearly many purposes that might be carried out by a land bank and a variety of approaches to the land-bank function. With these purposes in mind, it should be understood that this review does not claim to look at all land-banking activities, nor does it look in depth, or evenly, at the available experience. Rather, it is intended only to provide basic insights.

CHAPTER

8

THE U.S.
EXPERIENCE

This chapter reviews land-banking experience in the United States in the areas of industrial development, advance land acquisition for public facilities, housing and urban renewal, and open space. A land-banking operation has existed in Puerto Rico since 1962. Considering the nature of that activity, it is discussed along with experience in other countries in a following chapter.

All land-banking activities in the United States (except possibly Puerto Rico) are more aptly termed "project land banking," as defined in this study. The ultimate purpose of each activity—industrial, housing and urban renewal, public facility needs, and open space—differs. Industrial acquisition is concerned primarily with jobs and local tax revenues, housing programs with serving the housing needs of low- and moderate-income families, public facility programs with ensuring site availability, and open space with improving the recreational aspect of the quality of life. The following pages describe activities in each of these areas.

INDUSTRIAL DEVELOPMENT

This action briefly describes industrial land banks in Philadelphia, Pennsylvania; Baltimore, Maryland; and Milwaukee, Wisconsin. The basic purposes of these operations are to promote industrial development in order to provide for more jobs and tax revenues — in other words, to improve the city's economic state. The basic approach is the acquisition, site preparation, and resale of land for industrial purposes. Financing arrangements in each case have provided for tax exemptions, thus lowering interest rates and making development more attractive to the private sector.

In each of these cities, the industrial land bank has proved successful. This success establishes that local government intervention in the land market to promote (industrial) development is both desirable and profitable.

Philadelphia's leadership in planning for industrial development dates from the late 1940s, when it recognized the need to provide sites for industry suitable for single-story plants with adequate access facilities. The consequences of not planning for these needs, it was realized, would be loss of taxes and employment within the city. Preliminary work on planning for industry resulted in the creation in 1957 of the Philadelphia Industrial Development Corporation (PIDC), a nonprofit corporation whose purpose is to develop and assist private parties in developing industrial sites. Its board of directors is composed of major private interests such as banks, railroads, industry, and labor, as well as representatives of the city government. A number of interagency committees were also established to determine policy and timing of redevelopment.

Establishment of the PIDC was preceded by one year with the passage by the city council of a land-bank program. The major provisions of this act were[1] authorization of the city to transfer city-owned land to the Philadelphia Redevelopment Authority for industrial development and the setting up of an industrial redevelopment fund from the proceeds of sales of such land. "The PIDC is recognized as the most effective industrial development vehicle in any city in the United States"[2] concludes the study prepared prior to developing a corporation for Baltimore, Maryland, to further industrial development in that city.

Activities of the PIDC in industrial and commercial development include land development, financing, assistance to industrial developers, and promotion of development. Some statistics presented in the Baltimore study point out the effectiveness of the PIDC. Between 1967 and 1972, the PIDC was responsible for over 500 transactions, involving more than 30 million square feet of plant space and resulting in space for over 70,000 jobs, of which almost 40 percent were new.

The PIDC offers broad financing assistance for development of both privately owned as well as PIDC-owned land. This is carried out by two financing agencies associated with the corporation, the PIDC Financing Corporation and the Philadelphia Authority for Industrial Development (PAID).

PAID is central to the activities of the PIDC. Being a state instrument, interest from PAID transactions are exempt from federal income tax. Thus, projects can be financed at lower interest rates that are attractive to private developers. Certain restrictions are, however, imposed by the IRS on PAID financing, as follows: "PAID can create a tax exempt obligation of up to $5 million when capital expenditures within the community of the borrower (including the project in question) do not exceed $5 million during the six year period of three years before to three years after the project's borrowing. Otherwise PAID may create individual tax exempt obligations up to $1 million."[3]

Baltimore

The Baltimore Industrial Development Corporation (BIDC) was recently established as a nonprofit corporation composed of members from private and public sectors. It includes seven public officials appointed by the mayor, seven individuals designated by the business community, and six jointly chosen by the initial 14 members.[4]

The BIDC performs management responsibilities of the land-bank program for new industrial sites. These responsibilities include recommendation of sites to the city, site preparation and disposal, and coordination of the involvements of the public and private sectors. The BIDC relies on the Departments of City Planning, Public Works, and Real Estate in carrying out some of its functions. The actual purchase and disposal of properties is a municipal—not a BIDC—function carried out by the Board of Estimate.

The city has been authorized to issue $3 million in bonds (by referendum) for the purpose of furthering industrial and economic development in Baltimore. These funds will be used to acquire and improve land for eventual disposition for industrial use. The proceeds from sale of the land would not become part of a formal revolving fund, since annual reappropriation of the funds for the program require approval of the mayor and the city council. To the extent that these appropriations are made regularly, the program would be operating with what would in effect be a revolving fund.

The basic element that will make the land-bank program operate is a tax-exempt funding mechanism as described below. In 1965, the Maryland General Assembly established the Maryland Industrial Development Financing Authority to provide state guarantees for industrial mortgages. The Authority can "guarantee loans which cover the cost of land acquisition and site improvements, building construction and renovation, and machinery and equipment."[5] This guarantee can be used by the BIDC to obtain loans at favorable interest rates from private lending institutions. These loans can be used to acquire land from the city that was purchased for its land bank and resell or lease to a developer at a favorable rate. The BIDC interest on the BIDC loan is tax exempt, thus resulting in lower interest rates.

The land-bank program is designed to improve the local tax base, provide jobs, and retain existing industry as well as attracting new industry. Factors favoring the program in Baltimore include the existence of properly zoned but underutilized land, planned construction of freeways in the vicinity of selected sites, and the need for new industrial sites to serve firms displaced by urban renewal projects.

Milwaukee

In a report entitled The Land Bank: Eight Years of Industrial Development Progress, 1964-1971, Milwaukee's Department of City Development reports on its overwhelming success in the operation of its industrial land bank. The industrial bank was established to promote employment and generate new tax revenues. Six hundred new jobs have been created, and tax revenues far outweigh "losses" of taxes during the holding period. In the words of the report, "if we were to abandon the land bank program tomorrow, the City would still gain more than $1 million from the program."[6] This, on a total investment of $3,163,000. The total size of the land holdings in the Milwaukee Land Bank is relatively small (690 acres, of which approximately one-third has been sold or is under option), yet this first such land bank in the United States (according to the report) has had an important impact on Milwaukee.

In another report released seven months after the one just cited, an evaluation was prepared of the past and future expectations of the Milwaukee Land Bank. This report found that "although the strategy (of the 1960s) has served the City well, the present increased competition for industry strongly indicates that the program's current passive policies need to be revised in favor of more aggressive and competitive marketing efforts."[7] The recommendations reached into questions of administrative procedures, longer-term financing, and quicker reaction time to private development proposals, among many. The ends to be realized would include entrance into projects such as development of industrial parks, vest-pocket industrial renewal, incubator industries, and new town development. While these recommendations are largely tied to industrial needs (except for the new town proposals), it is clear that the Milwaukee experience exhibits the realities of economic development forces, city needs, and land-bank solvency.

ADVANCE LAND ACQUISITION FOR PUBLIC FACILITIES

The concept of advance land acquisition in the United States is by no means new. It was used in the nineteenth century by many

American cities, including the nation's capital. In more recent years, advance acquisition was used in the creation of the greenbelt new town (late 1930s). The Housing and Urban Development Act of 1965 contained a provision making grants available to cover interest charges for five years on lands purchased in advance for various public purposes. These grants were used for a variety of public facilities, such as school sites, street alignments, civic centers, airports, parks, and college sites by city, county, and metropolitan governments, among others.[8] Another important area of advance acquisition is the highway field. A good example of the active use of this technique is to be found in California, where there is a $30 million revolving fund to finance acquisition of land in advance of highway construction. Between 1962 and 1966, California spent $62,500,000 for advance land purchases. The Division of Highways estimated that if the same properties were to be purchased now (or at the time they were actually needed), they would cost some $380,500,000.[9]

A land-acquisition program began in Richmond, Virginia, during the 1940-1950 period. Three factors responsible for its initiation were the existence of a master plan to be followed in identifying site needs, the enactment of necessary legislation, and the establishment of a city real estate agency. This program is utilized in obtaining sites for a variety of public facilities. Needed sites are identified as part of the official map. The decision to purchase is not actually made until the landowner seeks a building permit to develop the land. This program has been reported to be financially successful and represents a case in which the planning process has aided advance acquisition as well as the reverse.[10]

Acquisition Programs

Advance land acquisition can be defined as a land purchase made before the point in time after which the completion date of a proposed project would be adversely affected. In general, this period would be at least two years, according to the Department of Transportation, and was considered to be three years in a questionnaire on the subject distributed by the National League of Cities.

As part of a study entitled "Advance Land Acquisition by Local Governments," questionnaires were distributed by the National League of Cities and the National Association of Counties to ascertain the extent to which acquisition programs are currently being used in the United States. Of the 144 (out of 306) questionnaires returned by cities, 73 indicated programs in advance acquisition and another 32 indicated occasional purchases. The results showed that 11 of the reporting cities averaged 6 or more acquisitions per year. The breakdown included two cities with 11-15 acquisitions per year and one city each with 16-25 and 26 or more acquisitions per year. The large majority of cities, then, do not have large programs. Only 18 counties reported having programs, however, the study concluded that "concerning counties, little can be said except that programs appear to be uncommon."[11]

Additional questions covered in the questionnaire included motives and purposes for undertaking land-acquisition programs and program operation. The following were given as major purposes for undertaking a program: avoiding rising land prices; obtaining the best location; and avoiding demolition.[12] Program purposes included those previously listed under HUD's interest payment program for advance acquisition as well as others. Under program operation, the questions were raised of availability of funds and legal restriction. With regard to the first point, one-third of the answers on impediments included insufficient funds. However, the study points out that the figure did not reflect the possibility that programs may not be initiated because of lack of funds. Funds that were utilized by various cities included capital fund reserves, unappropriated surpluses, capital fund revenues, special revolving land-acquisition funds, and bond issues. Both this study and others have given attention to legal issues. It can be concluded that (1) in certain cases present laws are sufficient and (2) recent interpretations of public purpose should allow for creation of laws to sufficiently meet requirements of advance acquisition.

In Montgomery County, Maryland, a program for advance purchases of school sites has been in operation since 1964. The ability to initiate the program is attributed to the interest of county residents in a superior school system and the high average income of these residents. The site selection procedure includes coordination with the Maryland-National Capital Park and Planning Commission (M-NCPPC) and the Washington Suburban Sanitary Commission (WSSC). The program is considered a success in many respects, including (1) financial viability, (2) reduction of uncertainties for homebuilders and buyers, and (3) provision of better school sites, all of which have a positive effect on the planning project. The success of the program is attributed to three factors. First, a positive political climate for developing a top school system; second, the general upward trend in land value (making it difficult to buy a site that would decrease in value); and third, the ability to realize economies of scale due to the size of the program and coordination with other county-wide organizations.

While the county has spent advance acquisition funds generally for park, open space, school sites, and county roads, as well as other public facilities, it has also recognized the special advantage of acquiring land for state roads to ensure that future transportation facilities will be available to county residents. Acquisition of state roads is reimbursed by the state with interest when the roads are built. Particular emphasis is put on roads because of the importance of transportation facilities and more specifically because (1) once an alignment for a road is announced and right-of-way acquisition begun, it is difficult and generally costly to change the alignment, even if land costs increase owing to construction of improvement in the right-of-way area, and (2) an announced alignment will generate speculative increases in land value, which will also increase the eventual right-of-way costs. For these reasons, it is desirable to have an advance land acquisition program to forestall such cost increase factors.[13]

In a related activity, Montgomery County, Maryland, received state approval in 1968 for the Public Facility Area Development Act. This act was initially termed the Land Bank Act, but was retitled to better reflect its scope and purposes.

The act provides that the Montgomery County Council can "purchase, hold, improve and dispose to public agencies and to private individuals and corporations for development according to an approved plan, real property needed to insure the orderly development of land adjacent to important public facilities."[14] The bill lists some 16 types of public facilities, including roads, interchanges, schools, and transit stations. The last item is particularly important, since a rapid transit system is being constructed in the Washington metropolitan area and includes two lines in Montgomery County.

The limits of the area adjacent to the public facilities subject to the bill depend on certain conditions. These are, primarily, the potential impact on the public facility of adjacent private development, or the area defined in an approved master plan whose development is desirable to implement plan concepts.

The act also directs that a public hearing be held on the designation of proposed public facility areas. Following this hearing, land may be acquired, a plan developed, further hearings held, and the land disposed of according to plan. The bill gives Montgomery County power to acquire land by all means except condemnation (that is, eminent domain). This power was also proposed in the initial draft of the bill. In disposing of the land, the county can include restrictions on future sale, lease, or assumption of incumbrances on the land subject to written consent of the county. Financing sources for the program can include taxes and issuance of special bonds. Acquisitions under this act can be carried out through the county's advance land-acquisition program for public facilities.

Advantages and Disadvantages

Advantages that can be derived through buying land in advance include the following:

1. Forestalling price rises, including increases due to natural upward trend as well as those due to conversion from rural to urban use.
2. Getting the best site.
3. Improvements in the pattern of related land uses. By advance announcement of the location of public facilities, private land development can be encouraged in the desired area. This can strengthen local planning and reduce uncertainties attached to other public and private decisions.
4. Improved procedures for site selection. This provides more opportunity for study and for coordination of site selection for all public facilities.
5. Return on temporary use. Land held for later use can be used in the interim for certain public or private purposes.
6. Acceleration of the renewal of declining areas by anticipating decline or accelerating it.
7. Provision of economies of scale through large-scale purchase and development.
8. Avoidance of demolition and relocation costs and attendant political problems.

In contrast to the advantages, the disadvantages are few but formidable. They are as follows:
1. Cost of capital, measured in terms of both interest cost and the lost "opportunity" for using the money in other ways
2. Lost property taxes
3. Management expenses of the program
4. Danger of acquiring unneeded properties
5. Danger of land price decreasing below acquisition cost

In developing fringe areas, the main body of advantages applies, including financial savings, site selection, and avoidance of demolition. In addition, an improved pattern of development might be realized in the fringe areas. The first three disadvantages—all monetary— also apply.

With regard to redeveloping areas, the application of the term "advance acquisition" is probably incorrect in that (1) acquisition is made for initiating a specific project immediately (although it may be staged over a number of years) and (2) central city renewal usually requires a write-down, as opposed to cost savings. Nevertheless, if a positive policy of ongoing city-wide redevelopment were undertaken, then conceivably a revolving fund and land bank could be created representing advance acquisition for future renewal. For developing areas, the main value of advance acquisition is in large cost savings.

URBAN RENEWAL AND HOUSING

Urban renewal provides one example of United States experience with public acquisition and disposition of land for the purpose of directing development. Review of the characteristics of urban renewal shows that it holds only limited significance for general land banking. Following, therefore, is a very brief listing of these characteristics and a comparison with general land banking.

Urban renewal (1) has a short-term orientation, (2) is aimed toward blight removal, (3) is concerned with redevelopment of small amounts of developed urban lands, and (4) is concerned with local problems in a single jurisdiction. It is also concerned with increasing land values in areas adjacent to urban renewal projects and with reducing project area land prices through the land write-down.

In contrast, general land banking is directed primarily toward the use of hitherto undeveloped land, is metropolitan oriented in terms of location and scale of development in related problems, and is concerned in general with reducing land costs through removal of "speculative increments."

In addition to the write-down, a basic tool of renewal is eminent domain. One source has noted the following as regards the use of eminent domain in the renewal process:

> ... Constitutional restriction on the exercise of the right to condemn a private citizen's property has created numerous, often cumbersome safeguards and procedures which must be followed before courts will permit condemnation. These procedures include public notice of hearings, the right to compensation determined (if demanded) by a court of law, the requirement that any taking of land be for a public purpose, and the requirement that the prerequisites of the statute be followed strictly.[15]

Finally, it has also been noted that a general land bank would encounter problems in utilizing land acquired by an urban renewal agency. That is,

> ... The complication results from the fact that the primary objective of the local public agency is redevelopment. Consequently, the agency is likely to be reluctant to market parcels to a land bank to be held for extended periods. Although considerable time may elapse in the urban renewal process, the actual land disposition contract typically calls for construction to begin within a relatively short time, say 60 or 90 days after the contract

is signed. As currently structured, urban renewal may be an attractive source of land for that part of the comprehensive land bank program which seeks to meet more immediate demands for housing types, but urban renewal may not be a source of land to satisfy long-range needs for future housing development.[16]

One final note can be added on the use of land banking for the purpose of providing low- and moderate-income housing. The Piedmont Triad Council of Governments has prepared a <u>Land Bank Handbook</u> focused on the acquisition and development of land for low- and moderate-income housing by a housing development corporation (HDC). Development of the handbook under that COG's land-bank project was assisted by HDCs in Winston-Salem, Greensboro, and High Point, North Carolina, which are actually engaged in the process of land banking for these purposes.

The handbook stresses the need for "a working understanding of fundamentals of determining the feasibility of the housing development as crucial to any successful HDC-Land Bank Program." This is seen in extensive materials on market analysis, site selection, appraisal of land, site improvement cost analyses, and so forth. The study also produced a computer simulation for acquisition, holding, and selling of land by land banks.

The report defines land banking as simply ". . . acquisition of land to be held for future use." In actuality the definition includes the optioning, buying, holding, and selling of land to private, non-profit, and public development corporations. The purposes, according to the report, are (1) to make land available for low- to moderate-income housing when and where needed, (2) to hold down housing costs, and (3) to assist housing sponsors without experience in the real estate market.

The report points out four reasons why an HDC should not get into the land-bank business. These are, briefly, (1) land for these purposes is and will be plentiful; (2) funds are unavailable or can be used better elsewhere; (3) the "service area" is too small to "support" a land-banking operation; and (4) land banking is risky, requiring professional skills.[17]

OPEN SPACE

As indicated in other parts of this chapter, public entities have been involved in the land market for the purposes of providing land for industry, housing and urban renewal, and advance acquisition of all types of public facilities. In a similar manner, much public

activity at all levels of government has gone into acquiring land for
a variety of open-space purposes. The scope of this study has not
permitted a review of existing experience in the United States with
open-space land acquisition. Undoubtedly, certain open-space acquisition programs are aimed at precluding development in certain areas.
Acquisition of open space could be a function of general land banking
if there is no clear delineation between land to be developed and not
to be developed, as provided, for example, in the Hawaii State zoning
ordinance.

PUERTO RICO LAND ADMINISTRATION

In 1961, Puerto Rico undertook the study of the processes affecting the supply and demand of land and the results and problems
associated with price change, speculation, and development. As a
result of this study, the Puerto Rico Land Administration (PRLA) was
established, with broad powers to acquire, hold, and dispose of lands
for certain purposes and in certain manners. Specifically, the law
allowed the PRLA to do the following:

> . . . acquire real property, urban or rural, which may be
> kept in reserve towards facilitating . . . development of
> public works and social and economic welfare programs
> . . . which may be undertaken by the Administration itself,
> by the Commonwealth of Puerto Rico or its agencies, and
> by private persons for the benefit of the above mentioned
> entities for the community including, but not limited to,
> housing and industrial development programs. . . .[18]

Thus, the PRLA may use the land for public and private uses and
dispose of the land to public and private developers. The study shows
that usable land was being bypassed only because of the inordinately
high prices, resulting in social, administrative, and economic problems.
More specifically, scattered development caused and would continue
to cause costs of public services and facilities, such as schools, roads,
water, sewer, open space, police, fire, and the like, which are beyond
the ability of governmental funds; increasing land prices would continue to price families with low and moderate incomes out of the market, thus placing a heavy burden on public housing needs; and increase
in land prices would increase overhead of industrial production, thus
raising the price of goods in Puerto Rico and affecting its competitive
standing in foreign markets.[19] Specifically, the legislative assembly
found as follows:

(a) that the Commonwealth of Puerto Rico is one of the most densely populated areas in the world; that urban lands, or lands adapted to urban development, are monopolized and kept unused by their owners, which creates an artificial shortage of land and raises its price at a rate higher than the raise in price of other properties and staple commodities; that the speedy raise in the price of land makes it impossible for persons of moderate or low resources to purchase land in appropriate areas, and forces such persons to build their homes outside the close-to-town areas and far from their places of work and other activities; that the raise in price of land makes for undesirable urban expansions, which in turn, creates serious financial problems to the Commonwealth and municipal government, as the costs of providing public services such as roads, water, sewer, public parks, public health, fire prevention and fire fighting, police vigilance, and others such as are necessary for the protection of life and property, so essential to the development of a community, increase several times; that the raise in the price of land increases the overhead costs of industrial and commercial enterprises, and, therefore, sets their product at a disadvantage in commercial competition locally as well as abroad; that the relatively speedy raise in the price of land increases differences in income, inasmuch as unused land in Puerto Rico, both urban and rural, is controlled, to a large extent, by a small number of persons; . . .

(c) that the raise in price of land also affects and prevents the implementing of the master plan and is a cause of worry for the public conglomerate and constitutes a serious problem, to control which available public funds may be put to maximum use, by authorizing the acquisition of private property whenever necessary;

(d) that it is in the public interest to avoid as soon as possible the excessive and disproportionate increase in the market price of land.[20]

The PRLA can acquire land through a variety of means, including use of eminent domain, and can dispose of land for a variety of public and private uses. It can establish conditions or limitations on use and can carry out development projects.

The Land Administration is authorized to acquire any real or personal property in any lawful manner. This includes general purchase, purchase by option, installment or public auction, or acquisition by lease, exchange, gifts or eminent domain. The private property so acquired may be kept in reserve to facilitate public work and social economic welfare programs, including housing and industrial development programs, recreational, beautification, and open space programs, and irrigation and reclamation programs. The only restriction imposed in maintaining this land reserve is that whenever land is acquired by condemnation for purposes of public work development or social welfare, such purposes will be carried out within 15 years from the date of acquisition.

In disposing of its property, the Administration is authorized to establish any conditions and limitations regarding its use or utilization as it may be necessary to assure the effectuation of the purposes of the Act. It is further authorized to sell land or interest therein at prices it considers reasonable in order to lower the cost of housing or to fulfill any of the other purposes of the Act. The Land Administration is further empowered to carry out by itself, or jointly with the agencies in the Commonwealth or the United States, or by means of covenants with private persons or entities, any programs, including housing projects, to ensure the most effective development and fullest utilization of land owned by the Administration, the Commonwealth, or its agencies.[21]

Financing of the PRLA includes issuance of bonds. The legislature has appropriated $20 million as an initial start for the land administration.

The governing body of the PRLA includes the governor of Puerto Rico; the heads of major departments, including Treasury, Public Works, Agriculture, Urban Renewal and Housing Corporation, and Economic Development Administration; and two appointees of the governor.

In general, the administration has acted as a "procurer" of land for various agencies rather than taking on projects. The general process involves a request by the agency for land to the Puerto Rico Planning Board. On board approval the PRLA acquires the land—often condemning lands around public facilities to inhibit price rises.

The PRLA often condemns land around public facilities to curb speculation and to capture the unearned, publicly created increment in value for the Commonwealth.[22] With regard to the price rise of properties designated for condemnation, the act provides that

just compensation shall be based on the market value of
the property without taking into consideration any increase
in such value due to the compensation project having been
announced and publicized and shall not include any real
increase by reason of the public improvement for expenditures made in the locality by agencies of the Commonwealth.[23]

The early emphasis on reducing land price inflation in the provision of land for public facilities has left the lower-priority problems of regional growth and urban sprawl. Thus it still appears that the "inflationary prices, leapfrog development, high transportation costs and expensive and inefficient public facilities will continue unless a program to induce more compact development can be implemented.[24]

This of course is an important commentary on the effectiveness of carrying out the two overriding goals of land banking—reducing land price inflation and orderly urban development—in that the state-of-the-art of land banking and planning is lacking. It has been acknowledged that part of the problem of promoting orderly development in Puerto Rico has been the lack of coordination between land-use and transportation policies. A project has now been established to challenge this problem. Known as TUSCAP (Transportation and Urban Settlement Combined Action Project), it uses the PRLA to implement policies. Results of the program thus far have been recorded to include the following:[25]

1. Between 1962 and 1970, more than 24,000 acres were acquired—much more than originally estimated as needed for this period—of which 6,100 acres were used by public agencies.
2. Construction of thousands of low- and moderate-income housing units resulting from holding down land prices.
3. Assistance to two new communities through land assembly.

In summary, the act establishing the PRLA was aimed at the general purposes of general land banking, permitting all means of land acquisition (including the use of eminent domain), with land to be used for all purposes, both public and private. Much more needs to be learned about the effectiveness of the PRLA in carrying out its responsibilities. From the available information, it would appear that the PRLA has directed its activities to functional rather than general purposes of land banking.

SUMMARY

This review of experience in the United States with respect to public intervention in the land market to carry out certain public objectives shows, first, that these activities, if taken together, would deal with all land-use types, public and private (private uses are provided for under urban renewal). If all of these activities were merged under an umbrella agency in one locality with a clear goal of providing land for all uses, this would constitute the intent of general land banking.

So far as the individual programs are concerned, this study has shown that industrial land banking and advance land acquisition for public facilities have proved highly successful. Although not discussed here, there is ample documentation to show that urban renewal has been relatively unsuccessful. Since open-space land acquisition is not actually a land-banking operation, it is difficult to talk in terms of success. It can be noted that, as stated in a study by the Metropolitan Washington Council of Governments,26 insufficient acquisition of open space inhibits the effectiveness of metropolitan plan implementation.

Certain characteristics of industrial land banking are particularly instructive for general land banking, including the use of nonprofit corporations and tax exemptions; representation on the boards of directors of labor, industry, banking, real estate; and the like. While there are many types of advance land-acquisition programs, few are large. The Montgomery County experience discussed in this study shows that certain factors furthered success, including rising land prices, economies of scale, and of course, adequate local funding.

The advantages of advance land acquisition for public facilities include forestalling rising prices, getting the best site, improve land-value pattern, better site selection procedures, and avoidance of demolition and relocation. The disadvantages, mainly financial, in large part explain the widespread lack of sizable programs.

While there is much more to be learned about the Puerto Rican experience, existing information tends to show that it has been more effective as a project land-banking activity for public facilities and low- and moderate-income housing than as a general land-banking program.

NOTES

1. Paul A. Wilhelm, "Industrial Development Planning," JAIP, August 1960, p. 218.
2. Subcommittee on Implementation of the Economic Development Loan Fund, <u>Establishing a Non-Profit Corporation to Administer the $3 Million Economic Development Bond Fund</u>, Report to the Mayor's Council of Economic Advisers, 1972, p. 3.
3. Ibid., p. 4.

4. Ibid., p. 5.
5. Ibid., p. 8.
6. Milwaukee Department of City Development, The Land Bank: Eight Years of Industrial Development Progress 1964-1971, Report to the Common Councils Committee on Economic Development (Milwaukee, Wis., 1972), p. 2 (of covering letter).
7. Milwaukee Division of Economic Development, Report of the Ad Hoc Advisory Committee on Land Use Strategies Concerning Industrial Development Policies and Programs for the 1970's (Milwaukee, Wis., October 1970), p. 1 (of covering letter).
8. U.S. Department of Housing and Urban Development, Office of Resources Development, Advance Acquisition of Land Application Log for 1969-1970 (Washington, D.C., 1970).
9. Donald C. Shoup and Ruth P. Mack, Advance Land Acquisition by Local Governments (New York: Institute of Public Administration, 1968), p. 15.
10. Ibid., pp. 85-97.
11. Ibid., p. 16.
12. Ibid., p. 17.
13. Ibid., pp. 65-84.
14. Maryland Senate, Public Facilities Area Development Act, 1968, Sec. 26A1-26A4, Montgomery County Code, p. 1.
15. Piedmont Triad Council of Governments, Land Bank Handbook (Greensboro, N.C., September 1972), p. K-2.
16. Ibid., p. K-3.
17. Ibid., p. A-1.
18. Richard P. Fishman and Robert D. Gross, "Note, Public Land Banking: A New Praxis For Urban Growth" (23 Case W. Res. Law Rev. 897, 918. 1972), p. 916.
19. Ibid., p. 918.
20. Puerto Rican Land Administration Act of May 16, 1972, no. 13, Statement of Motives.
21. P. R. Laws Annual, title 23, § 311f (j) (1964).
22. Fishman and Gross, op. cit., p. 922.
23. Ibid.
24. Ibid.
25. Ibid., pp. 922-923.
26. Metropolitan Washington Council of Governments, The Changing Region (Washington, D.C., 1969), p. 48.

CHAPTER

9

FOREIGN EXPERIENCE

As stated in a report prepared for the New York State Urban Development Corporation, "none of these policy recommendations (such as those described elsewhere in this paper) for public land banking, including those specifically addressed to the New York State Urban Development Corporation are accompanied by any supporting evidence such as review of contemporary European and Canadian experience or analysis of alternative strategies for maintaining land inventories."[1] That report concluded, with regard to foreign experience, that it is evident from the study of planning systems in Western Europe (Netherlands, Scandinavian Countries and Great Britain), western Canada and Puerto Rico that, to ascribe advanced systems of urban land development entirely to public land ownership based controls would be incorrect. These policies must be viewed in light of other aspects of development guidance and control. This finding, at the minimum, places land banking in its proper perspective as only one part of an overall approach to guiding urban development

In gaining an understanding of the possibilities for general land banking in the United States, it is highly desirable that a thorough study be made of experience with this technique in other countries. Such a study is not possible in the scope of this work.[2] The purpose of this chapter is to highlight some of the characteristics of land banking in other countries. From this brief review it will be seen that strong emphasis is placed in other countries on the integration of local, regional, and national policies with regard to taxation and land development, plan review, and land-use controls. There are also specific lessons to be learned concerning sale and lease policies, acquisition policies and financing, and the structure of land-bank entities.

COMPARATIVE EXPERIENCE

The following discussion is based largely on the study by the Center for Urban Development Research mentioned earlier and is divided into the categories of land search, acquisition, inventory, disposition, organization, and financing for land banking. The discussion includes experience in the Scandinavian Countries, the Netherlands, Canada, Great Britain and Puerto Rico.

The basis for the land-bank program in Puerto Rico dealt with problems of land price and development, as discussed elsewhere in this study. In Western Europe, crowded conditions, a relative land shortage, and war damage generated acceptance of public intervention in land ownership. In Britain and the Scandinavian countries, there is the political theory that all land belongs to the Crown; and in western Canada, land reform in the early 1900s and the depression that led to the takeover of "tax-foreclosed lands" helped form the basis for land banking in that country.

Search

In Western Europe, approval of local and regional development plans by the national government is generally a prerequisite to acquisition and/or development. Also, national and local taxing powers regarding real property transactions, land development, and municipal services play an important role in the coordination of urban growth plans.

The Scandinavian countries, the Netherlands, and Great Britain have achieved coordination of public land ownership with systems of taxation, public preparation of land for building, master planning, and land-use regulations, the last of which pertains to the control of open spaces, including agricultural land. In Sweden and Great Britain, land acquired under land-banking operations can be used for general development, while in Denmark land can be used for roads and infrastructure but not for public housing.[3] "Nearly every municipality in the Netherlands has developed an active land banking program, administered by an independent grounds department."[4] This has resulted in development nearly identical to original plans due primarily to conditions on land disposition. In Denmark explicit actions are taken to control land speculation through land banking. Specifically, "Copenhagen offers its own land at low prices and in competition with the private landowners when private demand seems excessive."[5] "Israel has established a national land acquisition fund to prepare land for agricultural settlement and to develop land for housing and industrial purposes. The fund leases its land for forty-nine years to public or private bodies, with provisions for extension and inheritance. Rentals amount to four percent of land value and must be paid annually. Land values are reviewed every seven years."[6] "In Canada, public land ownership programs are shaped through the coordination of municipal with provincial policies."[7] The federal government has delegated the power of land assembly to the provinces, which in turn have delegated this authority to municipalities. Land policies in municipalities are subject to review by the provinces and are coordinated by the local and regional planning and development procedures.

Acquisition

Except for Puerto Rico (which works closely with local governments in its acquisition activities), the national governments of the Scandinavian countries, the Netherlands, and Great Britain have delegated land-acquisition powers to "local" governments or semipublic corporations, permitting them to plan and implement land development according to local characteristics of timing, location, economy, and population considerations. In the Scandinavian countries and Great Britain, negotiation is most commonly used for acquisition, although condemnation power is available. In Denmark and to some extent Norway and Sweden, land is purchased on the open market. In Sweden, expropriation is slow and expensive. In Norway, "special state bonds" can be offered to landowners for their land. These bonds mature in 10 years, and if held for this period, the land sale is exempt from a capital gains tax.

Inventory

The amount of municipally held land varies among cities with land banks. As noted elsewhere in this study, Marion Clawson has estimated that perhaps 60 percent of the land in the area of land-bank operation should be held by the land bank for an effective program. By 1966, 74 percent of the land within Stockholm was owned by the city. In Denmark, three cities hold more than two-thirds of their land, and five cities hold more than half. In Oslo, Norway, more than 45 percent of the land is city-owned, with most under long-term lease. In Finland, land holdings for different cities will serve between 2 and 20 years of future growth needs. Some localities in Canada hold land for 10 to 20 years of expected growth, while in Puerto Rico little land is held in reserve.

Disposition

In some locations in Scandinavian countries and in the Netherlands, land is disposed of for 40- to 100-year leases, depending on use. In Denmark and Norway, disposal is mostly through sale. Some interesting deed restrictions are found in Canberra, Australia, and in Millwood in Edmonton, Canada. In Canberra, leases include use restrictions, standards of maintenance, and provision for reversion in cases of noncompliance. In Millwood, a home buyer who sells his property cannot buy another home within the development for the following five years.

One study, entitled <u>Urban Land Policy—Selected Aspects of European Experience</u>, has concluded the following with regard to the "argument" as to whether sale or lease is the better method for land disposition:

> Whether land should be resold after it has been acquired by government seems to be a moot question. The trend seems to be toward retention of ownership and transfer by leasing. This method provides government the opportunity to control future uses within a minimum of legal complications and to retain the gain from increases in value. On the other hand, record keeping for a large number of leased properties is no small responsibility and requires considerable expense to perform satisfactorily. There also can be speculation and profiteering in leased land to illegal subleases unless careful control is maintained. If the intent is to retain the full gain for the State, such factors can be detrimental. Israel, where 92.5 percent of the total land area is State-owned, has decided that administration of leasing procedures must be improved in order to avoid such problems.[8]

Organization

In the Scandinavian countries and the Netherlands, land-bank agencies are generally departments of the municipal government. In Norway there are joint corporations of municipalities with public or quasi-public corporations. In Stockholm the land-acquisition fund has been delegated to an autonomous municipal corporation called STRADA. Other land-bank functions in Stockholm are carried out by a city agency. Such functions include policy, pricing, disposition, coordination with the national housing agency, selection of builders, supervision of land preparation, and financing. The purpose of the separation is to improve efficiency and ensure confidentiality in negotiations with private landowners.

In Finland, a private, nonprofit corporation has been established for development of new towns. In Great Britain, a public corporation (British Development Corporation) has been established to carry out land-banking activities. The Puerto Rico Land Administration (PRLA) has total control over its properties and activities, including use of funds, but can work jointly with the Commonwealth of Puerto Rico, federal government agencies, and private enterprise. The PRLA was designated in 1970 to control all land acquisition and disposition for Commonwealth agencies.

Financing

In the Scandinanvian countries, municipalities can tax incomes of individuals as well as levying other taxes and fees in order to finance land acquisition. They can also receive national and other grants and loans. In the Netherlands, the national government provides loans at the market rate for 75 years on land and 50 years on buildings. The British Development Corporation can borrow from the treasury at below market interest rates for a 60-year period. Private financing can also be used. Alberta, Canada, receives federal loans and can also use its own borrowing instruments. The PRLA receives grants and loans from the Commonwealth, can issue its own financing instruments, and can seek federal loans and private financing. Most of the PRLA's funds have been in the form of Commonwealth grants.

NOTES

1. Center for Urban Development Research, Public Land Acquisition for New Communities and the Control of Urban Growth: Alternative Strategies (Ithaca, N.Y.: Cornell University, March 1973), p. xvi.
2. For detailed discussions of foreign experience, see Gordon Edwards, Land, People and Policy (West Trenton, N.J.: Chandler Davis, 1969), pp. 47-73.; U.S. Department of Housing and Urban Development, Office of International Affairs, Urban Land Policy— Selected Aspects of European Experience (Washington, D.C., 1969); Urban Land Research Analysts Corp., Municipal Land Reserves Policy: An Analytical Study of Foreign Experience (Lexington, Mass., 1968).
3. Center for Urban Development Research, op. cit., p. 4.

4. Richard P. Fishman and Robert D. Gross, "Note, Public Land Banking: A New Praxis For Urban Growth" (23 Case W. Res. Law Rev. 897, 1972), p. 911.

5. Ibid., p. 912.

6. Ibid.

7. Center for Urban Development Research, op. cit., p. 4.

8. Ibid., p. 37.

CHAPTER

10

**LAND-BANKING
PROPOSALS**

This chapter describes a number of recent proposals for land banking and related activity in the United States. The sources of these proposals include recommended legislation at the state and federal levels; governmental studies at the city, county, subregional, regional, state, and federal levels; other governmental studies that have touched upon land banking; and recommendations by certain professional planning societies.

The variety of sources of these proposals shows that broad-based interests exist in public intervention in the land market in the form of land banking. The diverse proposals can be seen to establish the concept of land banking as ranging from advance land acquisition to an important facet of a national urban growth policy. These proposals include recommendations for both general and special land banking. The latter includes recommendations for advance land acquisition for public facilities (as discussed earlier in this book); new towns, housing, and other uses.

In the proposals reviewed, primary emphasis for the level of government that would carry out land banking is placed at the metropolitan and state levels. The federal role, where discussed, is generally seen as one of coordinator or financer of land-banking operations.

Within the review of existing proposals, the specific issue that stands out most is the political and social implication of land banking. In essence, the fear of low-income housing and minority groups in suburban areas appears to be a central factor inhibiting serious consideration of land banking as a means of controlling development.

The following pages present a brief summary of these proposals This is followed by a more detailed description of each proposal.

LEGISLATIVE PROPOSALS

Proposals dealing directly or indirectly with land banking have been brought before the New Jersey and Hawaii state senates and the U.S. Congress. To date, no action has been taken on any of these proposals.

The bill in Hawaii would establish a state development corporation (SDC) that would also administer a state land bank. The land bank would apply only to nonurban districts in Hawaii (agricultural, conservation, and rural). Within these districts, the land bank would provide land only for low- and moderate-income housing and associated commercial facilities. Another function of the SDC would be to provide land for various uses in urban areas. Rules could be established by the SDC that would supersede certain existing local regulations; the SDC would also have "quick-take" powers and could establish a revolving fund.

The legislative proposal in New Jersey would establish a state planning commission that would carry out a land-banking operation for public uses, new communities, and guidance in critical areas. An interesting provision of this bill would have a landowner wait two years after his announcement to develop the land in an area designated for use by the commission. This bill never got off the ground because it went against home rule and because of fear of low-cost housing and minority groups in the suburbs, according to one of the bill's sponsors.

In the Catholic University Law Review and in proposed legislation, Senator Vance Hartke has outlined the position of land banking as an important aspect of any national urban growth policy. The Hartke bill would establish, among other things, state and metropolitan planning agencies and state and metropolitan development agencies. The development agencies would be required to have as purposes the provision of low- and moderate-income housing; renewal; and development and redevelopment of industrial, manufacturing, and commercial facilities. While the bill permits land acquisition and proposes federal grants and guarantees for loans and the revolving fund, it places a limit of 10 percent on the amount of grant funds that could be used in any one year for land acquisition. In discussing the proposed legislation with an aide to Senator Hartke (Bruce Johnson), it was learned that an eminent domain provision was not included in the bill owing to fear of a public reaction to "socialization" by the proposed agencies and the possibility of politicizing of the land bank for integration of suburbs.

GOVERNMENTAL STUDIES AND PROPOSALS

In a proposal for establishing general metropolitan land banking and a federal urban development bank (Urbank), Charles Haar, former assistant secretary of the Department of Housing and Urban Development, presents the basis for federal intervention in establishing land banks. The rationale concerns (1) the proper use of federal funds and (2) public policies regarding population, housing, environment, and the like. Certain of his recommendations are based on a study by the Urban Land Research Analyst Corporation (ULRAC) for the Department of Housing and Urban Development. Such recommendations, as well as Haar's rationale, are embodied in part in Senator Hartke's recommended legislation, described earlier. Haar's recommended land bank would be general in nature and concerned with all facets of metropolitan development and redevelopment, public and private land uses, and public and private development.

An interesting note may be added on the ULRAC study. In addition to other recommendations, the study recommends the acquisition of neighborhood-size areas by a land-bank agency for redevelopment. This approach ignores not only the historical difficulties of urban renewal but also the present power of existing residents in these areas that would be displaced. The ULRAC report also recommends not only that all the land on the periphery of the city should be publicly owned but also that the best mechanism would be some sort of overall metropolitan authority or state, multistate, or federal entity. It is instructive to see the generality of the proposals developed under this HUD study.

The Maryland Planning and Zoning Law Study Commission was established to review existing state planning and zoning laws and make legislative recommendations. Available documents indicate that the commission was to undertake a feasibility study for state land banking dealing with public facilities. According to the executive director of the study commission, this feasibility study was not undertaken for political reasons. The interim recommendations included state authorization for establishment of land reserves; however, the final report did not include such recommendations.

A report prepared by the Baltimore Regional Planning Council entitled "A Land Bank for the Baltimore Region—A Suggested Approach for Implementing the Master Plan," was concerned primarily with public uses and the possibility for private development. This study was not followed up because it was "branded as socialism," according to a source close to the council, and there were fears of low-income housing being forced on the suburbs and of possible abuses of a land-purchase program.

The subject of land banking was briefly reviewed by the Maryland-National Capital Park and Planning Commission (M-NCPPC), a bi-county planning agency for Montgomery and Prince George's Counties, Maryland, and by Montgomery County, Maryland. The M-NCPPC study was highly in favor of the concept of land banking, or "land reserves." The review by Montgomery County for new towns concluded that it was infeasible to be carried out by the county. That review also noted the need for an amendment to the state constitution to clarify the question of the use of eminent domain for such an undertaking for new towns.

OTHER GOVERNMENTAL STUDIES

A report by the American Society of Planning Officials (ASPO) reviewed five major reports. One finding of this review was that in one manner or another all these reports supported the concept of land banking. The National Commission on Urban Problems, better known as the Douglas Commission, was concerned primarily with federal assistance for housing. However, this study also recommended state action regarding land banking for general development, dealing with sprawl, protection of highway interchanges, and capturing gains in land values for the public.

A study by the Advisory Commission on Intergovernmental Relations, entitled "Urban and Rural America Policies for Future Growth," recommended land-banking activities by state and local governments for creation of new communities as part of the implementation of a national urban growth policy. Finally, a report by the Canadian Federal Task Force on Housing and Urban Development recommended what the ASPO report considered the most radical view on land banking, which called for general land banking by all municipalities in Canada.

The American Institute of Planners (AIP) and the American Institute of Architects (AIA) have both made recommendations concerning land-banking activities. A policy statement on new communities issued by the AIP concerning public land acquisition was as follows:

> The American Institute of Planners has issued a policy statement on new towns in which they recommend a more active governmental role through the route of public land acquisitions. In areas of current rapid growth they urge local governments, and especially counties, to consider establishing development agencies . . . having the power to acquire land, prepare it for development, dispose of it for development in accordance with the detailed plan . . .[1]

85

The American Institute of Architects was in agreement with the AIP on metropolitan development agencies. Recommendations of the AIA were picked up in Senator Hartke's bill and call for broad responsibility and power concerning development and redevelopment in all parts of metropolitan areas, with a recommendation of federal assistance for the initial acquisition of one million acres of land in 60 of the nation's largest metropolitan areas. The AIA report also recommended state urban development corporations such as now exist in New York State.

DESCRIPTIONS OF PROPOSALS—LEGISLATION

Hawaii

In 1973 a bill (Senate Bill 1350)[2] was introduced in the Hawaii state legislature by State Senator John J. Hulten and others to create a state development corporation (SDC) and state land bank (SLB). The bill was not acted upon in 1973 and is expected to be acted upon in 1974, according to correspondence with Senator Hulten.[3]

The broad purposes of the act are to provide land for needed housing in order to minimize the needs for state public assistance, and to provide the land for industrial, commercial, and manufacturing in urban areas.

The SLB would be administered by the SDC. Land acquired for the land bank would be used for residential and associated commercial uses. Such bank land could only be acquired in rural conservation and agricultural districts upon development of a statewide plan for this purpose for acquisition of private properties. For such land, the SDC would be empowered to adopt rules and regulations concerning planning, zoning, and the like, that would supersede the existing regulations. Sale or lease to developers would be by bid, with the award based on design concepts, aesthetics, and other criteria, as well as price. Finally, as regards the land bank, a revolving fund can be established to support the SLB activities. In essence, then, the land bank would be essentially for a single purpose—housing— in more or less developing areas. No attempt is made through the land bank to guide urban development or reduce land prices. The primary function of the land bank would be in providing housing for low- and moderate-income families.

In urban areas, the primary emphasis is on providing land for low- and middle-income housing and land for industrial, commercial, and manufacturing uses in more or less blighted areas. Senator Hulten has termed the purposes of the bill (in materials accompanying the bill) as follows: "Under this plan, urban growth and development would be controlled by the community instead of, as at present, by the land owners, speculator, or developer."[4] Within the bill provision is made for consideration of local policies and plans, and land so developed must conform to some degree with local plans. However, there is no explicit statement that the corporation would develop strategies aimed at effectuating an overall plan, of curbing sprawl, of lowering land prices, or the like, which are characteristic of general land banking.

It is nevertheless instructive to briefly review some of the structural, financial, and legal characteristics of the proposed SDC. The directors would include heads of four of Hawaii's state departments and five appointees of the governor. An advisory council for urban development would be established, consisting of broad representation from commerce, industry, finance, construction, housing, and labor. Land acquisition would be by all means, including condemnation and disposition through all means (including lease, generally up to 99 years).

Financing would be through grants and bonds or notes secured by projects and revenues. A reserve fund would be established to cover each year of succeeding principal and interest. No provision was made, however (other than for court action), as a further guarantee of such debts, such as the faith and credit of, or appropriations from, the state or other sources. The SDC would be exempt from state and local taxes on land and bonds, but the state must pay property taxes on land withheld specifically for industrial use.

An interesting provision is that the land disposal must generally be made without public notice, sale, or bidding, except that the disposal details must be published and public hearings held. Provision is also made for the SDC to take possession upon entry and filing of an order with the court if the court so deems.

Finally, similar to a provision in the act establishing the Puerto Rico Land Administration, the bill provides that "no award of compensation shall be increased by reason of any increase in the value of real property caused by the actual or proposed acquisition, use or disposition by the corporation of any other real property for corporate purposes"[5] (Section 13f). This would, of course, have the effect of reducing land speculation, at least in areas where the SDC is quite active.

In a draft paper entitled <u>New Policies to Control Land Use in Hawaii</u> (prepared for Hawaii State Senator John Hulten), Herbert J. G. Bab, an economics consultant in California, puts forward an interesting and potentially far-reaching proposal for land banking that differs from land-banking proposals that advocate the "normal" operations of the private land market.

The chief characteristic of the proposal is that only land purchased by the land-banking agency could be rezoned; that is, "the rezoning of privately owned land will have to be prohibited,"[6] thus preventing developers from choosing development sites for "higher" uses.

Other characteristics of the proposal would include the following: Land would be sold for one- and two-family housing and condominiums, but leased for all other uses to guarantee control of future reuse; land-sale prices would include costs of public facilities, infrastructure, and markups to prevent excessive profits of subdivision (except for low-income housing); rents of housing or lease sites would be tied to profit rate and mortgage interest rate and reviewed yearly to account for increased cost.

Site selection would be the responsibility of the state land-use commission and planning department. These vested powers and the requirements cited earlier would have the effect of carrying out the following purposes of the land bank: public ownership as prerequisite for all rezonings; all land (except as noted) eventually owned by the land bank; public costs allocated to the developers; low-income housing promoted; and reuse controlled.

New Jersey

In 1969 a bill[7] was introduced to the New Jersey legislature for the purpose of guiding development in critical areas, reserving land for certain public uses, and purchasing land for certain purposes. This bill would also establish a state planning commission to carry out these responsibilities.

The state could purchase land for conservation, recreation, transportation, education, health, and welfare "purposes" and for new communities. Further, the bill would establish a land-purchase fund that the commission or other designated state agencies could use for purchasing land. This land could then be sold or leased for desired purposes or sold if the original purposes are no longer desired.

To complement this concept the commission would develop an official map designating future-use areas, which would be acquired. If an owner proposed to develop land in these designated areas, the state could put a two-year waiting period on development; during this period it would decide whether or not to purchase.

Through correspondence with one of the sponsors of this bill, former Senator Willard C. Knowlton, it was learned that the bill "never got off the ground."[8] The reasons for this, as stated by the senator in a letter to the author, were as follows:

The bill failed to muster support for two main reasons: (1) it went against the "home rule" principle, which in New Jersey, although not to be found in the State Constitution or in any statute, is the equivalent of a matter of theological dogma and just as infallible. Consequently, the bill immediately ran into the opposition of the New Jersey League of Municipalities even before it was printed up; (2) much of the opposition to the bill came from the suburbs, especially the affluent and wealthy ones. They feared the intrusion of low-cost housing in their towns, the overcrowding of population which they thought might ensue, the rise of real estate taxes which a growing population might cause, additional costs for municipal services, such as police, fire protection, refuse disposal and the like, and, perhaps, more importantly, the fear of the intrusion of minority groups.[9]

The Hartke Bill

Senator Vance Hartke (Democrat, Indiana), in a 1973 article in the Catholic University Law Review, presented an outline of his thoughts on a national urban growth policy. In this publication he picked up on a number of recommendations presented in an AIA task force report described elsewhere in this study and made a specific recommendation for metropolitan land banks. Hartke stated that this would be ". . . an integral component of a national growth policy . . ."[10] and that it would be an aim of his recommended national development bank and national development corporation. The basic function of the former would be the provision of capital funds for depressed areas and would operate similarly to the World Bank. The functions of the corporation would be as coordinator of metropolitan, state, and regional development corporations and to act as a "developer of last resort."

Hartke describes the functions of the metropolitan land bank as providing metropolitan authorities with federal assistance for land acquisition, management, and disposal. The senator notes certain benefits of land banking that have been identified in most sources on the subject, such as advance acquisition for public facilities, curbing sprawl, capturing incremental land values, and improved management and control of the land market.

On March 19, 1973, Senator Hartke introduced S. 1286, "A Bill to Provide for National Growth Policy Policy." This lengthy bill provides for many of the characteristics described in the article mentioned earlier, and for others as well. It would seek to establish state and metropolitan planning agencies, state and metropolitan development agencies, regional growth planning and development commissions, and a national growth planning council. The latter would, among other things, supervise and coordinate the activities of the metropolitan, state, and local agencies.

The planning agencies would be empowered to develop growth policy plans, control large-scale development and development around new communities, prohibit growth inconsistent with the plan, manage federal grants to all local jurisdictions, and acquire interests in real property.

In section 205d, the bill provides that no more than 10 percent of grant funds in any one fiscal year to such agencies may be used for acquisition of interests in real property.

Under Title V, state metropolitan development agencies would be established that must include in their purposes provision of low- and moderate-income housing; renewal; and development and redevelopment of industrial, manufacturing, and commercial facilities. The agencies would also be supported by federal guarantees of obligations and revolving funds. Interestingly, the bill provides no connection of the development agencies with the planning agencies, which, as noted earlier, are also authorized to acquire real property.

It is clear from the 10 percent limitation on the planning agencies that this bill does not intend to support large-scale land banking with federal funds. From the description of the development agency, it appears that this agency is oriented toward project rather than growth planning. Passage of this bill and initial federal funding could clearly represent, however, a significant start for metropolitan land banking.

DESCRIPTIONS OF PROPOSALS—
GOVERNMENTAL STUDIES

Federal Role

In submitting a proposal for legislation at the federal level in support of land banks, Charles Haar offered the following philosophy in justification of federal intervention: First, it is the responsibility of the federal government to see to it that federal funds used for development of the urban infrastructure—roads, sewers, water, open space, and the like—are used efficiently. This implies that local land-use plans and programs be implemented and that overlapping and unnecessary duplication of expenditures be reduced. Second, federal policies dealing with the distribution of population, development of new housing, improvement to the environment, elimination of poverty, and so forth, justify federal intervention at the local level to guarantee that these policies will be carried out.[11]

Haar feels that while the federal government has acted as an aid to the private market in providing data on population, employment, the market, and the like, it must now go further in ensuring that federal funds are used properly. To this end, he suggests that incentives are needed for reorganization of local government structures to form metropolitan governments, which can deal effectively with urban problems, and that the federal government can be effective in "eliminating legal and technical impediments to the free and easy use of the land."[12]

In essence, Haar suggests that it is the federal role as both innovator and experimenter to take the lead in development of land banks as a means for effectively organizing for and dealing with urban development. To this end, he recommends metropolitan land banking to "provide Federal assistance to metropolitan authorities to acquire, manage, and dispose of land according to conditions of the metropolitan plan."[13] Major elements of the proposal include the power of eminent domain for site assembly, the power to spend public moneys on the facilities required to achieve the desired form of structure, and the power to dispose of land to private and public developers in accordance with the metropolitan development plan.

Haar identifies a number of special purposes to be carried out by the land bank, including advance land acquisition for public purposes, avoiding the expenses of urban sprawl, as an instrument for perfecting the land market, as a key tool for orderly development, and to recapture land values created by government activities.

Maryland Planning and Zoning Law Study Commission

In 1966, the Maryland General Assembly established the Maryland Planning and Zoning Law Study Commission for the purpose of making a comprehensive review of the state planning and zoning laws, and to recommend revised legislation to the Legislative Council.

One subject considered for study by the commission was a land-bank system for Maryland. An outline for this study cited Montgomery County, Maryland, activities in advance land acquisition; Baltimore's interest in an industrial land-bank program (which has come about recently, as noted elsewhere in this book); and the Baltimore Regional Planning Council's initial report, <u>A Land Bank for the Baltimore Region</u>, all of which are discussed in this study.

The outline described the purposes of the study and the feasibility study to determine if the land-bank system for Maryland is justified. The feasibility of land-value and purchase-time optimization models was also to be explored.

In a discussion[14] with Ann Kramer, executive director of the study commission, it was learned that the commission's approach to the land-bank concept dealt primarily with land acquisition for public facilities. It was also learned that the study was not undertaken owing to political issues associated with the concept of land banking. Nevertheless, the commission's recommendations did include a limited reference for land banking in the form of land reserve, as explained later.

The commission identified three alternatives for guiding development in Maryland. The first was to maintain the status quo. It was observed that ". . . it is clear from the overall view that the State as a whole and especially the metropolitan communities have not been able to achieve the goals of planning through land-use regulation now available . . ."[15] The second approach was amending the state planning, zoning, and enabling legislation. Such recommendations were made in the commission's final report. The last approach was a comprehensive new system of development regulations. The system envisioned would include departments of development located in the executive branch of government, a development code containing all land-use regulations (including authorities to participate in land reserves), uniform procedures for authorization and guidance of development, provision in state law for regional planning agencies, and authorization for the establishment of land reserves at all levels of government to permit advance acquisition of lands for public purposes.

The commission stated with regard to the land-reserves aspect that "the physical planning process at all levels of government would be synthesized into precise plans and the real estate needs for all public programs would be identified in sufficient scale for property acquisition to proceed."[16] With respect to the "comprehensive development system," the commission stated as follows:

> Once the local, regional, and state planning and development organization and departments were established, and once the codes and plans were adopted, private and public development would take place only if consistent with adopted plans.[17]
>
> Under this system, elected officials would also have authority commensurate with their responsibilities for the quality of the environment.[18]

As noted earlier, the land-banking study was not undertaken. In the <u>Final Report on Legislative Recommendations</u>, no recommendations were made regarding land banking or land reserves.

Baltimore

In 1967 a report was prepared by the Baltimore Regional Planning Council entitled A Land Bank for the Baltimore Region—A Suggested Approach for Implementing the Regional Plan. The report is a brief description of the advantages of this approach and the procedures needed to bring it about. As described in the report, the land bank would acquire land for public programs but ". . . might also be used to acquire land for selected types of private development, especially where large-scale land assembly is involved."[19] In a discussion with a representative of the council, it was learned that the proposal did not get beyond this point.[20] Nevertheless, it is instructive in a number of ways. First, the very consideration of the idea by a regional planning agency (as by the Maryland Planning and Zoning Law Study Commission) shows that there is genuine interest in the land-banking concept on a metropolitan scale. Second, in listing the steps needed to implement a land-bank program, the report recognizes two important prerequisites. One is the improvement of the planning process to the point at which specific land-purchase needs (sites) can be identified for all public programs in the region, and the other, that U.S.-guaranteed bonds would be necessary to establish a revolving fund for the program. With respect to the first point, the report identified the need for two models to supplement judgment on land purchases. These are a purchase-time optimization model and a land-value prediction model. Such models are not currently available as planning tools in the United States. With respect to the guarantee of bonds, a discussion with the author of the report revealed that HUD had indicated that such guarantees would probably not be allowed by the Treasury Department in the coming year (after 1967), which helped discourage use of the concept by the Regional Planning Council.[21]

Montgomery County, Maryland

As noted earlier, Montgomery County, Maryland, and M-NCPPC, of which Montgomery County is a part, gave some consideration to the idea of land banking or land reserves in brief papers. The M-NCPPC report, entitled The Land Reserve System, concluded that ". . . a land reserve system should be initiated as soon as possible . . ."[22] with purposes that might include development of public facilities, industrial and commercial development, and new towns.

Montgomery County, which (as noted earlier) has been involved in land acquisition for many years, has investigated the idea of land banking with respect to new town development in the vicinity of public facilities. While the view of the county's involvement in developing new towns is that it is not feasible at present, it is nevertheless stated that "public sponsorship of new towns could promote urban growth of a desired character, location and timing far more effectively than can direct means of zoning and subdivision regulation, even when these police power controls are vigorously supported by capital improvements programming.[23] Some of the benefits noted in that report that could be realized by government acquisition and assembly of new town sites include the following: (1) economies in transportation and other capital and operating expenditures; (2) environmental amenities, especially in the preservation of open space; (3) lower-cost construction for housing and public facilities; (4) superior site design and better arrangements of land uses; (5) ensuring the availability of sites for various uses at reasonable prices; (6) providing opportunities for small businessmen by removing delays and the need for large initial capital outlays; and (7) recouping values of public expenditures in population growth.

The two problems that are cited as facing the county's involvement in land banking for new towns are the need for a constitutional amendment to ". . . eliminate any ambiguity about the uses of eminent domain for land for private development . . ." and the "boldness" of such an undertaking for the county. The latter "problem" can, of course, be read to include the entire array of considerations in new town planning.

REVIEW OF A MAJOR REPORT

In the ASPO report Toward a More Effective Land Use Guidance System, the recommendations of five major reports on guiding the use of land are examined. The reports are the following:

The Advisory Commission on Intergovernmental Relations (ACIR), Urban and Rural America: Policies for Future Growth

The National Commission on Urban Problems (Douglas Commission), Building the American City

The American Law Institute, A Model Land Development Code (Tentative Draft No. 1)

The Canadian Federal Task Force on Housing and Urban Development, Report of the Task Force on Housing and Urban Development

The American Society of Planning Officials, New Directions in Connecticut Planning Legislation

In introducing these reports the ASPO paper states that "because of the national stature of the reports and because they agree in many respects in their findings and recommendations, they may lead to fundamental changes in the theory and practice of land use guidance."[24]

The reports generally treat land as being in one of three phases of use—developed, redeveloping, or developing. The primary technique recommended for developed areas is zoning. For redeveloping areas, recommendations include protection of usable areas and stimulation of new development—the latter assisted through public land assembly, as is done under urban renewal. In developing areas a guidance system is recommended that is aimed toward flexibility in allowing communities to have the maximum information available prior to land-use decisions.

In discussing land-use guidance techniques for developing areas, the ASPO report identifies seven major bases for the recommendation. These are (1) shaping regional and community growth, (2) curbing urban sprawl, (3) ensuring an adequate supply of land for certain kinds of private development, (4) acquiring land for public purposes, (5) protecting land with unique characteristics, (6) lowering the cost of public improvements, and (7) regulating relationships between landowners. Noticeably absent is the objective of capturing the increase in land value brought about by public investments. (Sylvan Kamm has noted, for example, that while a public investment may add to the land value, it may be only one part of the increase, with additional increases due to private investment.)

Methods suggested for guidance in developing areas include planned unit development, floating zones, conditional rezoning, compensatory payment, and public acquisition and disposition to ensure certain types of development. According to the ASPO report, "one of the most important recommendations of the (five) reports is that local governments should be empowered to intervene directly in the development process by purchasing or condemning land and reselling or leasing it to private developers subject to conditions."[25] The ASPO report indicates that this concept is referred to in the reports as land banking, which it defined as "the acquisition of land several years in advance of urbanization." It is noted that most reports would support the right of urban government to acquire and dispose of land at any time to achieve certain objectives. The following paragraphs present brief descriptions of three of those reports.

Douglas Commission

The Douglas Commission report produced some 149 recommendations generally concerned with methods for reducing housing costs and "opening up" the suburbs to lower-income families and minorities. These recommendations were grouped into housing programs, housing and building codes, urban government structure and state-local government relations, taxation, and orderly urban development, among others. The land-banking proposal was presented in the last category as one of seven major recommendations.

As stated in the report, (guidance) "techniques suggested in the preceding section (of the Douglas report) on undeveloped and built-up areas have been modifications and extensions to the existing system of non-competitive regulations." The report states further that

> It is becoming apparent, however, that many public land use objectives will not be achieved by complete reliance on police power techniques. At the present time, many desirable objectives are not even formulated unless it appears possible to achieve them through the exercise of the police power. And all too often attempts to apply the police power approach have resulted in failure to achieve public objectives, and have been accompanied by substantial inequities and abuses of power. The Commission believes that the time has come for government to assert its legitimate concern with urban development by the use of techniques necessary to accomplish public objectives. In many situations, this requires that the government actually obtain land—through purchase or eminent domain—and that regulation be supplemented by compensation to private property owners. Where actual purchase will result in the government's recapturing increases in land values for the public, government should deem this a legitimate function and added incentive for direct action."[26]

Thus, land banking is recognized in this report as a very specialized form of regulation to be applied in certain situations. The commission's recommendations on land banking encompass state authorization for this function and provision of federal assistance for land acquisition. These specific recommendations of the commission are as follows:

> Recommendation 7(b)—State Authorization for Land Banking.
> The Commission recommends that State Governments enact legislation enabling State and/or local development authorities or agencies or general purpose governments to acquire land in advance of development for the following purposes: a) assuring the continuing availability of sites needed for development; b) controlling the timing, location, type and scale of development; c) preventing urban sprawl; and d) reserving to the public gains

in land values resulting from the action of government in promoting and servicing development. At a minimum such legislation should authorize the acquisition of land surrounding highway interchanges. At such times that development of such land is deemed to be appropriate and in the interests of the region, such land could be sold or leased at no less than its fair market value for private development in accordance with approved plans. Whereever feasible long term leases should be the preferred method of disposing of any public land, and lease terms should be set so as to permit reassembly of properties for future replanning and development. Legislation should specify a maximum period that such land may be held by the public before lease or sale.

Recommendation 7(c)—Provision of Federal Assistance for Land Acquisition.

The Commission recommends that the Congress enact legislation establishing a Federal revolving fund to facilitate the purchase of land by local governments in owner-initiated compensation proceedings and as part of direct-purchase programs, with the Federal contribution to be returned to the fund upon disposition of the property. Furthermore, the Congress should enact legislation authorizing the Department of Transportation to assist States in acquiring land surrounding federally assisted highway interchanges."[27]

The commission report states that there are two areas of public policy that appear impossible to carry out without public purchase. These concern physical development and what is termed the impact of regulations on land value. The latter refers to the resultant windfalls to certain property owners due to regulations. The commission feels that public purchase would not only remove this inequity but also ". . . obtain the speculative profit for the public."[28] The commission believes, however, that the policies related to phycical development are more important and provide a rationale for experimenting with land banking. The principal goals identified concern development of "major new subcenters," industrial areas (as in the PIDC, BIDC, and Milwaukee experience), and highway interchanges, which the commission stresses heavily and for which it recommends a federal program through the Department of Transportation.

ACIR Report

A recommendation of the ACIR Report would have local governments guide the development of new communities. Three types of methods are suggested—planned unit development, high-intensity sectors, and reserve land. The reserve lands would serve recreational needs, expansion requirements, and as greenbelts. The land reserve would be used essentially through "withdrawals" from the land bank.

The report recommends "enactment of State legislation to provide for chartering State and local land use development agencies." This agency would basically deal with land acquisition, assembly, and improvements for large-scale and new communities land purchase. This is seen by the ACIR as ". . . a major method of implementing state and local urban growth policies."[29] The specific recommendations dealing with this subject are as follows:

> Recommendation 4. Enactment of State legislation to provide for chartering State and local land development agencies.
>
> The establishment of State land development agencies empowered to undertake large-scale urban and new communities land purchase, assembly, and improvement would provide a major method of implementing State and local urban growth policies. Specifically, such agencies could: 1) acquire land by negotiations and through the exercise of eminent domain; 2) arrange for site development and construct or contract for the construction of utilities, streets, and other related improvements; 3) hold land for later use; 4) sell, lease or otherwise dispose of land or rights thereto to private developers or public agencies; and 5) charter local or regional land development agencies. All such powers should be exercised in accordance with, and in furtherance of, the State urbanization plan.[30]

The report recommends a variety of financing methods, as follows:

> The agencies' operations could be financed as appropriate, through direct appropriations, charges and rents, grants, sales of land, and borrowing, if authorized. Borrowing authority could be granted on a revenue basis in anticipation of land sales and rents. Revenue from land sales and rent could provide a major source of income and a significant part of the operations of State land development

agencies could be on a revolving fund basis after an initial appropriation of working capital, supplemented only as needed by subsequent direct appropriations or borrowing.[31]

Canadian Task Force Report

The ASPO report terms the Canadian Task Force Report the most radical in its recommendations because it states that "municipalities or regional governments as a matter of continuing policy, should acquire, service, and sell all or a substantial portion of the land required for urban growth within their boundaries."[32] The report cites both planning and cost efficiency bases for this proposal. Cost efficiency arguments include elimination of speculative increment of land value, thus lowering the cost of raw land; economies of scale if land is assembled and disposed of on a large scale; reduced costs and risks to developers by removing the holdout and assembly problems; and relaxed local development standards, which tend to raise costs.

AIA RECOMMENDATIONS

In 1972 the AIA prepared a task force report on urban growth. This report represented the thinking of many of the most distinguished people in the field of urban planning. In that report was the recommendation for national and state development corporations and metropolitan planning and development agencies (proposed in Senator Vance Hartke's legislation, discussed earlier in this study). The development agency would deal with development and redevelopment in all parts of the metropolitan area. The agency would have powers over the location and timing of infrastructure elements (roads, water, sewer, etc.) as well as other urban "shapers," such as airports, open space, federal buildings, and ". . . other public investments that influence economic development." This would also include "authority over the locations for low- and moderate-income housing and the control of major zoning decisions in the metropolitan area." Further, it would have the power of eminent domain for acquisition of land and vacant and quasi-vacant areas, deteriorating areas, land in the path of development, and raw land at the periphery of metropolitan areas. (The Douglas Commission recommends either lease or sale of land.)[33]

Significantly, the report recommends that a plan for development of acquired land would be prepared "once such land is acquired."

This is similar to the approach in Stockholm, Sweden, which is considered responsible for the level of success in that city. The report also states that this agency should be electorally responsible, but does not discuss this idea further. At the state level, the AIA report recommends state urban development corporations like that in New York State. At the federal level, the report recommends assistance to metropolitan areas based on the requirements of establishing metropolitan development agencies. Also, significantly, it is recommended that the federal government provide funds for immediate acquisition of one million acres on the peripheries of the 60 largest metropolitan areas in the country. The estimated cost of this land is $5 billion—well within our grasp. It is instructive to note that implementation of the latter recommendation would have to be directed toward implementing present plans rather than becoming part of a well-thought-out overall land banking program for these metropolitan areas.

SUMMARY

In the preface it was stated that this study does not deal with alternative approaches to controlling growth—though such a process is clearly necessary in considering general land banking as one approach. Many of the proposals reviewed here represent, to a degree, the consideration—and rejection—of alternatives without governmental involvement in the land market. The call for governmental involvement beyond that already existing, as discussed under "Existing U.S. Experience," is clearly indicative of a trend that can be expected to result in more governmental activity in the land-development process.

The various proposals place before us some thoughts with regard to political problems of the land-bank concept and some aspects of land-banking approaches. With regard to the former, there can be expected cries of forced low- and moderate-income housing and minority groups in metropolitan suburbs, fear of corruption in the land-purchase program, fear of widespread use of condemnation of private property, loss of home rule, and higher real estate taxes and municipal service costs. Such fears may not be unfounded.

Running through the grain of the proposals discussed is the provision of land for low- and moderate-income housing in all parts of metropolitan areas. Corruption is clearly a realistic possibility, and the use of condemnation by a land-bank program can be expected in many cases. In terms of general land banking on a metropolitan scale, there clearly must be some loss of home rule. Even in project land banking for specific purposes, the feared loss of home rule is not unfounded, particularly where the state is the land-bank entity.

As discussed elsewhere in this study, general land banking can be expected to result in higher real estate taxes on private holdings. The impact of subsidizing low- and moderate-income housing under this type of land-bank operation might also result in higher taxes and service costs. In sum, whether under a project or a general land bank program, these fears must be given serious consideration.

As far as the approach to land banking is concerned, the various proposals have recommended state land banks as well as planning and development agencies at metropolitan, regional, state, and federal government levels. The range of powers and/or responsibilities that would be given to the land bank include determining the location of low- and moderate-income housing; overriding local regulations; land disposal without public notice, sale, or bids; land disposal by sale or lease; improving land for development; condemnation with quick-take provisions; imposition of a waiting period on private developers during which the land bank decides whether to acquire the site; rezoning only by the agency; acquiring land for all governmental needs and control of the location and timing of infrastructure and other public facilities; control of major zoning decisions; management of federal grants to all jurisdictions; and operation within all parts of the metropolitan area as developer or land dealer. This array of powers and/or responsibilities certainly suggests a basis for concern about the desirability of general land banking on a metropolitan scale if not with project land banking.

Certain proposals call for land banking on a metropolitan scale but would appear to be project oriented, since the proposals call for metropolitan development agencies although they would operate in all parts of the metropolitan area for development and redevelopment, possibly including industrial and commercial uses as well as low- and moderate-income housing and public facilities. The proposals thus indicate very limited support for general land banking on a metropolitan scale. The reasons for this lack of support may be seen in the issues identified in this study.

NOTES

1. American Institute of Planners, Policy Statement on New Communities, Adopted by Board of Governors, May 5, 1968.

2. Hawaii Senate, Ways and Means Committee, A Bill for an Act Establishing a State Development Corporation and Land Bank, 7th Legislature, 1973 (S.B. No. 1350).

3. Information in a letter to the author from John J. Hulten, State Senator, State of Hawaii, April 19, 1973.

4. John J. Hulten, "Proposal for Controlling Urban Growth and Eliminating Land Speculation," ca. March 1973, p. 1.

5. Hawaii Senate, op. cit., sec. 13f, p. 36.

6. Herbert J. G. Bab, "New Policies to Control Land Use in Hawaii" (unpublished draft), chap. 3, p. 1.

7. New Jersey Senate, S. B. No. 803, May 12, 1969. Introduced by Senator Willard B. Knowlton and Richard J. Coffee.

8. Information in a letter to the author from Willard B. Knowlton, former State Senator, State of New Jersey, May 14, 1973.

9. Ibid.

10. Senator Vance Hartke, "Toward a National Growth Policy" (22 Cath. U. Law Rev. 231, 1973), p. 928.

11. U.S. Congress, Senate, Committee on Government Operations, S1286, A Bill to Provide for National Growth Policy Planning, 93d Cong., 1st sess., March 19, 1973, p. 928.

12. Ibid., p. 930.

13. Ibid., p. 932.

14. Interview with Ann Kramer, former Executive Director of the Maryland Planning and Zoning Law Study Commission, May 10, 1972.

15. Maryland Planning and Zoning Law Study Commission, A Review and Discussion of Development Trends in Maryland (Baltimore, Md., January 1968), p. 80.

16. Ibid., p. 88.

17. Ibid.

18. Ibid., p. 89.

19. Regional Planning Council, A Land Bank for the Baltimore Region, a Suggested Approach for Implementing the Regional Plan (Baltimore, Md., June 1967), p. 7.

20. Interview with Randy Whittle, Baltimore Regional Planning Council, June 2, 1972.

21. Ibid.

22. Robert P. Duckworth et al., The Land Reserves System: An Approach to the Possible Application to the Bi-County Region, Working Paper no. 13, (Maryland-National Capital Park and Planning Commission, 1968), p. 23.

23. William H. Hussman, Memorandum to County Manager: Advance Land Acquisition and Land Bank (Montgomery County, Md., 1968), p. 34.

24. David Heeter, Toward a More Effective Land Use Guidance System: A Summary and Analysis of Five Major Reports, Planning Advisory Service Report no. 250 (Chicago, Ill.: American Society of Planning Officials, 1969), p. 1.

25. Ibid., p. 58.

26. National Commission on Urban Problems, Building the American City (Washington, D.C., 1968), p. 250.
27. Ibid., p. 251.
28. Ibid., p. 252.
29. Advisory Commission on Intergovernmental Relations, Urban and Rural America: Policies for Future Growth (Washington, D.C., 1968), p. 161.
30. Ibid., p. 162.
31. Ibid.
32. Hector, op. cit., p. 58.
33. American Institute of Architects, A Plan for Urban Growth: Report of the National Policy Task Force (Washington, D.C., 1972), p. 10.

CHAPTER
11

**SUMMARY AND
CONCLUSIONS:
ISSUES IN GENERAL
LAND BANKING**

Jacob L. Crane has said of land banking:

> Here we have one of the greatest unknowns of city building. It remains an unknown up to now particularly because we are not clear in our heads about what might be best as both a <u>technically feasible</u> and <u>politically feasible</u> method.[1]

This is an understatement, to say the least.

General land banking on a metropolitan scale as an approach to metropolitan plan implementation in the United States—in concept, in relation to existing institutions, in practice—has been shown in this study to be questionable in its ability to carry out its goals. It requires a heavy payment in institutional change, would be fraught with operational difficulties, and has a number of largely undefined impacts, particularly on the land market and price rise of land.

This study has touched upon many aspects of land banking—goals; relation to plan implementation; legality; structure; land acquisition, holding, and disposition practice; and the historical background. It has also tried to define what land banking is and should do. The keynote of all this is the pervasiveness of the land-bank concept. It is pervasive in the requirements it places on changes in existing approaches to metropolitan plan implementation; in the political implications of its position in the governmental structure and its requirements for metropolitan "cooperation"; and in its impact on the private land market as well as on the concept of private land ownership.

Metropolitan land banking is pervasive in its ground rules—provision of land for all use types, public and private; no prior specification of use; acquisition of a substantial amount of metropolitan area land; operation in all parts of the metropolitan area; competition with the private market; expectation of substantial use of eminent domain with quick-take powers; as a frame of reference for all other land-use controls; requiring a high subsidy, at least in its early years of operation—these are but a few of the implications of metropolitan land banking. (Note that whether these rules must be part of a metropolitan land-bank operation depends on the definition of a land bank's role in an actual metropolitan area.)

Yet these possible characteristics and the issues summarized in this chapter must be viewed against a background of lack of effective metropolitan plan implementation and the prospects for the effectiveness of alternative approaches.

As shown in the review of land-banking proposals, there is much belief in the idea that bringing about change requires public intervention in the land market. Experience in the United States with project land banking for industrial needs and public facilities has shown that public intervention can be successful. The brief review of foreign experience suggests that much can be learned about the issues facing general land banking.

In sum, while this study has shown that general land banking on a metropolitan scale is not at present an effective means for controlling growth patterns, this concept is too important to dismiss. If it is to be tested in the United States, there must be a metropolitan land-banking experiment. It is only within a real context that the significance of the issues raised herein can be found.

This experiment would be designed to define what general land banking on a metropolitan scale can be in a specific metropolitan area, to dissect the issues and determine how to deal with them, and thus to determine if there is a feasible approach to implementation. Through this experimental approach, consideration can be given to the structural approaches identified in Chapter 5 (aggregation of jurisdictional general land banks and aggregation of metropolitan project land banks) as well as the structural approach of a metropolitan-level general land-bank entity.

This experiment must begin with selection of an area "most likely to succeed" at metropolitan land banking. Criteria for selection should include minimal racial problems, few jurisdictions or a metropolitan government, previous progress in plan implementation, moderate size, and a highly developed, comprehensive plan and planning process.

The groundwork for land banking in such an area would include development of an adequate data base (and models) for testing land-banking feasibility and development of alternative approaches to a land banking operation—structure, activities, powers, responsibilities, financing, and so forth.

All this must presume, first, an agreement in principle on the part of metropolitan area officials to look at land banking, and second, a thorough metropolitan forum on the alternative approaches and their implications in light of a promise of sustained federal assistance to remove the possibility of fiscal turmoil. (This presumes the need for a subsidy based on assumptions of high initial costs with little or no return, and difficult financing. A preliminary study for the financial feasibility aspect of a land-bank program would determine the need for and size of a subsidy program.)

If this process can be accomplished, then a metropolitan land bank can be initiated, monitored, and evaluated. If not, metropolitan land banking will remain simply a recommendation in the professional literature.

A discussion of the issues involved in general land banking follows.

CONCEPT

The central conceptual issue in general land banking is the conflicts among its primary goals of controlling growth and regulating land price as well as capturing capital gains from public investment and regulating land use. The specifics of these conflicts were discussed earlier in this study.

The growth strategy would have the land bank follow closely the comprehensive plan, while the price strategy would have the land bank act as speculator to obtain the greatest return. From the multi-objective viewpoint of urban planning, it is not sufficient to operate a land bank by criteria of economic efficiency. In practice, there must be a trade off between these goals.

INSTITUTIONAL ISSUES

Planning

Present United States planning works on the basis of the private market, either following governmental leads such as location of infrastructure or in restrictive means such as zoning or penalties for not following government guidelines, as under federal grants. Land banking is radical in calling for government intervention to direct what will happen—the location, type, and timing of development.

The adequacy of the present planning process to guide a land bank may be viewed from several perspectives, including the degree to which the comprehensive plan reflects metropolitan desires, its ability to identify specific land needs, and the viability of the metropolitan plan. In addition, as identified in this study, many changes may be required as prerequisites to a land-bank program—changes in existing land-use controls dealing with location and timing of infrastructure, zoning, and taxation; in planning processes; and in the governmental and institutional structure for planning.

Place in Government Structure

Whether metropolitan land banking can be carried out within a structure other than metropolitan government is one of the most basic issues in whether it should be attempted in the United States. In reviewing present governmental arrangements, the only possibility that has been held out so far for immediate use is some form of public corporation. Can such an entity adequately grapple with such issues as where to place low- and moderate-income housing, decisions on competition with the private market and between land-use types, substantial use of eminent domain, and the like, as well as the objectives of individual jurisdictions in contrast to metropolitan goals? Beyond this, how would the land-bank entity be related to a metropolitan planning agency? Would it be a subsidiary carrying out the plan, or would it be independent, interpreting the plan? It should also be noted that other structural arrangements such as aggregation of jurisdictional general land banks or metropolitan project land banks may be attempted as structural approaches.

POWERS

Existing metropolitan plan implementation in the United States relies on cooperation among area jurisdictions. Land banking will require more than cooperation in terms of its area and purpose of operation and the types of changes and powers needed to support the program. This raises the more fundamental question of how much governmental control is acceptable and should be centralized in one agency.

Powers that appear to this author to be necessary to a land-bank operation include the following (this, of course, is not intended to be an exhaustive list):

1. to operate in all parts of the metropolitan area
2. to keep land in reserve for a period consistent with its goals
3. to acquire and dispose of land for all types of land uses

4. to improve land for development
5. to acquire land without prior specification of use
6. to determine the type of use to which land will be put
7. to be solely responsible for acquisition of land for certain major structural public facilities
8. to use the right of eminent domain for land acquisition
9. to specify a waiting period restricting private owners until the land bank decides whether to acquire a site
10. to dispose of land by sale and lease
11. to carry out development projects
12. to establish conditions in disposition of land
13. to borrow money, issue bonds, and receive grants and other sources of funds
14. to establish a revolving fund

Certain other powers are desirable for a land-bank agency, including the following:

1. Certain zoning responsibilities. (Alternatives might include metropolitan-level zoning powers, final decision on major zoning cases, and in area jurisdictions, the ability to override local zoning regulations.)
2. Quick-take powers.
3. A policy-level voice on the timing and location of major infrastructure elements.
4. Power to determine the location of low- and moderate-income housing.

POLITICAL CONCERNS

There is need for political accountability on the part of the land bank in areas such as land transactions (including the possibilities of corruption and secrecy); administration of its powers; lease negotiation; land acquisition, holding, and disposition decisions; goal achievement; metropolitan equity; location of low- and moderate-income housing; use of eminent domain; home rule; and fiscal impact. Responsibilities in such areas requires clearly defined means for political accountability.

FISCAL IMPACT AND EQUITY

Considering the importance of property taxes in supporting local activities, the fiscal impact is among the most important concerns of a land-bank operation. Also, the need for a fiscal equity plan requires consideration of equity in distribution of land use (and possibly land value) as well as costs and revenues of the land-bank operation.

LAND MARKET AND PRICE RISE EFFECT

Little is known about the operation of land markets or the decision processes of the various "actors." Yet an understanding of these factors is necessary to the operation of a land-bank program. The land bank must obtain a large amount of data on land transactions, must have means (models) for data evaluation, and must be able to effectively predict land values and supply and demand elasticities as a basis for operation and financial management.

There is a basic unknown with respect to the nature of the impact of a land bank on land prices in the private market. It is possible that the reduced supply of land by virtue of the land-bank program, as well as higher expectations by the private market, will raise the price of private land and therefore each additional parcel acquired by the land bank. To what extent will this occur? What effect will it have on the metropolitan economy? And to what extent will this be moderated by subsidy of the program? It has also been hypothesized that the price rise effect will result in the land bank's not being able to carry out its primary goals or social objectives.

OPERATIONAL ISSUES

Land Acquisition, Holding, and Disposition and the Decision Process

There are complex relationships between, on the one hand, at least the following: land-bank strategies regarding acquisition, holding, and disposition of land; total land holding and free reserve at any given time; pace of acquisition; land-ownership concentrations; and financial arrangements; and on the other hand, at least the following: metropolitan physical and economic characteristics; land supply and demand elasticities; price rise of land-bank and private land; the effect of the inflationary cycle; and taxation. These and other factors must be considered in the land bank's decision process as well as in the decision to attempt land banking and in evaluating its effectiveness.

Scale of Operation—How Much Land?

This is a central issue in land-banking desirability, financial feasibility, and ability to carry out land-banking goals. Available research has shed little light on how much land is needed, though Clawson did venture an estimate of 60 percent of the land in the area of land-bank operation. This suggests not only that the program will be expensive but also that it will operate on a large scale and take a number of years to reach the desired level.

Free Reserve

Associated with the scale of operation is the amount of free-reserve land—that is, land available for "immediate" development and not including land committed for public facilities, under lease, or not prepared for development. If the operation is to be effective in competing with the private market, whether under a growth, price, or combined strategy, it must have sufficient free reserve to sustain competition in order to convince the private market that its policies will prevail. There thus needs to be a means for determining the level of needed free reserve at any given time, and the ability to have it available.

Eminent Domain

The use of condemnation by a land bank may be central to its operation either as a tool or as a lever in negotiation. A number of problems may be seen in the use of eminent domain, including public opposition, lengthy court cases, and precedents for higher prices. Unless this power is available (and possibly with quick-take provisions), the land bank may be unable to acquire land at a reasonable price and at a reasonable pace.

Sale Versus Lease

Issues associated with sale versus lease are detailed in Chapter 7. The importance of sale or lease policies depends on the type of land use, scale of development, and administrative questions, among others.

LEGALITY OF LAND BANKING

This subject more aptly stands in a category of its own. However, the specific legal aspects may dictate certain operational consequences for a land bank in terms of what it can and cannot be involved in. As an example, while it may be able to acquire land for all uses without prior specification, it may be in conflict with laws dealing with acquisition for certain kinds of public facilities.

FINANCING

The financial feasibility of a land bank is one of the central issues in the feasibility of land banking. A few of the problems of financing, such as continuing funding availability, conflict between financial and land-bank objectives, and sources of funds, have been discussed in this study. An intensive financial feasibility study, considering alternative approaches, is a necessary prerequisite to undertaking land banking. One of the many questions that must be addressed is, If a subsidy is required for a land-bank program, is this an acceptable premise for operating a program?

EVALUATING THE OPERATION

There must be means for a full evaluation at regular intervals, such as every five years, to determine the effects of the land-bank program relative to expectations and changing conditions. Such evaluations are necessary if we are to learn about the practicality of land banking in the United States.

As a final note it must be stated that the preceding list of issues is intended to consolidate many issues identified in this study. Examination of these issues would result in a finer breakdown of each, thus generating more specific concerns. In addition, other issues not identified in this study, conceptual, institutional, operational, or other nature, will certainly develop as a more detailed study of land banking is undertaken in the context of an actual metropolitan situation.

NOTE

1. Jacob L. Crane, <u>Urban Planning—Illusion and Reality</u> (New York: Vantage Press, 1973), p. 121.

APPENDIX: QUESTIONNAIRE ON THE PUERTO RICO LAND-BANKING EXPERIENCE

RELATIONSHIP TO URBAN PLANNING

Purposes

1. The article discusses a number of reasons for establishing the Puerto Rico Land Administration (pages 918-919) and the purposes to be carried out (page 916). The following is a list of major purposes of land banking identified in the literature. Could you comment on the degree to which you view these as functions of the PRLA and the relative amount of "effort" thus far placed upon each?

   a. Shaping regional and community growth.
   b. Curbing urban sprawl (also, has much previously bypassed land been filled in).
   c. Ensuring availability of land for various types of public and private land uses.
   d. Protecting land with unique characteristics (e.g., environmental, historical landmarks).
   e. Lowering the costs of public services.
   f. Lowering the costs of public facilities.
   g. Regulating the relationship between landowners (in terms of that part of the functions of zoning).
   h. Capturing increases in land value for the public.
   i. Reducing land price rise.
   j. Reducing land speculation
   k. Development of vacant sites and redevelopment within highly developed urban areas.

Metropolitan Plan, Planning Process, Public Policies, and Land-Use Controls

2. In general, to what extent has the functioning of the PRLA been effective in implementing the various aspects of the San Juan Area Plan?

The article referred to in the first paragraph of the questionnaire is Richard P. Fishman and Robert D. Gross, "Note, Public Land Banking: A New Praxis for Urban Growth," Case Western Reserve Law Review, 1972, pp. 916-923. The abbreviation PRLA is used throughout the questionnaire for Puerto Rico Land Administration.

3. What type of plans does the PRLA prepare for its use in making decisions on land acquisition, holding, and disposal?

4. What effects have the activities of the PRLA had on the concepts of planning and on the preparation of the San Juan Metropolitan Plan? Do these signify the need for new approaches in planning and the preparation of metropolitan plans?

5. What major changes in public policies affecting the planning process have come about as a result of the activities of the PRLA?

6. What changes in planning and public policies have had a major effect on the activities and purposes of the PRLA?

7. Have differential effects been observed on metropolitan development and land price rise in the portions of the San Juan metropolitan area where the PRLA is more active versus the portions where there is little activity by the PRLA?

8. How, and to what extent, have PRLA decisions been coordinated with and affected by public decision making in the following functional categories?
   a. Water trunk line locations.
   b. Sewer trunk line locations.
   c. Transportation facility locations (I have noted pages 922 and 923 regarding the need for better coordination in this area).
   d. Open space.
   e. Housing—low, moderate, and middle income.
   f. Industrial development.
   g. Commercial development.
   h. Public facilities (I have noted page 921, last paragraph, regarding this area).

9. In what ways has the planning process in San Juan been instrumental in affecting decisions of the PRLA? What improvements are needed in the planning process to assist the PRLA in being more effective?

10. Suburban land conversion is affected by a variety of public policies. Some of those identified in the literature as needing vast improvement are listed here. How much have these been affected since the inception of the PRLA, how important are they to PRLA operations, and what are the expectations for their improvement?
    a. Tax law changes regarding capital gains on land sales.
    b. Assessment and portion of market value used for taxing purposes.
    c. Zoning, flexibility and level of government administering.
    d. . Public facilities coordination with development areas
    e. Data on land sales and supply and demand.

11. In what ways are the development policies of governmental units in the San Juan metropolitan area considered in the decision process of the PRLA?

12. Does the PRLA experience imply the need for metropolitan government in order to carry out metropolitan land banking?

13. Does the land-banking process, as practiced in the San Juan metropolitan area, hold implications for metropolitan equity in the distribution of tax revenues and the location of land uses?

14. An important issue raised regarding metropolitan land banking has been that it would hasten integration in suburbs through provision of low- and moderate-income housing. Is the social make-up of Puerto Rico such that this is not an issue in the operation of the PRLA?

OPERATIONS

15. What are the basic characteristics of the decision processes concerning the following:
   a. Land acquisition (which land to acquire, when, and for what purposes).
   b. Land holding (average length of time of holding, interim-use policies).
   c. Land disposition (which land to dispose of, when, for what purposes, and when to start disposal procedures relative to planned land use).
   d. What are the major attributes and problems associated with these decision processes?

16. To what extent are land acquisition, holding, and disposal policies used as a means for balancing the private land market?

17. How much free-reserve land—that is, land that can be disposed of relatively quickly—is needed to balance speculative activities?

18. What is the physical distribution of land thus far acquired, held, and disposed of? That is, how much land has been acquired in developing areas around San Juan? What portion is
   a. developing area land
   b. within developed area of San Juan
   c. development fringe of San Juan metropolitan area
   d. other parts of Puerto Rico

19. a. Are data available showing the amount of land acquired and disposed of each year (possibly by location and purpose) by the PRLA since its inception?
   b. To what extent does the PRLA prepare land for disposal?
   c. Have many large-scale projects been undertaken by the PRLA?

20. The following methods of acquisition were listed in the article (page 920) as available to the PRLA. To what extent has each been used, and what problems and advantages are associated with each? Are there other methods that are desirable?
    a. general purchase
    b. purchase by option
    c. installment or public auctions
    d. acquisition by lease
    e. exchange
    f. gift
    g. eminent domain (also see next question)
    h. other desired methods

21. Four major issues have been identified in the literature associated with the use of eminent domain in a large-scale land-banking operation. To what extent have these issues been significant for the PRLA?
    a. Lengthy court procedures.
    b. High court awards setting a precedent, thus making future use of eminent domain more difficult.
    c. Political opposition to extensive use of eminent domain.
    d. Availability of the power of eminent domain as a factor in negotiations.

22. On page 922, first paragraph, it is stated that ". . . the land administration often condemns surrounding land (around governmental projects) to curb speculation, and to capture this unearned, publicly created increment in value for the Commonwealth."

How often and at what scale of acquisition (amount of surrounding land acquired compared to size of project) has this been applied? Have any significant problems been associated with this technique?

23. On page 922 the footnote (118) to the quote in the previous question indicates that "just compensation" shall be based on market value without consideration of increased values due to announcement of the project or public improvements.

Has this provision been used on a regular basis, and are there any associated problems?

24. What methods are used for management of lands being held? What are the significant problems of land management and holding (particularly costs)?

25. It has been pointed out that land disposal by sale provides a constant flow of money, thus reducing the cost of the operation, while disposal by lease makes later redevelopment easier. What methods are used by the PRLA, to what extent, and why?

26. What types of conditions are generally attached to land disposal (related to type of land use, disposal method, land user—public or private)?

27. What effects have these conditions had on the ability of the PRLA to dispose of land?

LEGAL FACTORS

28. Have there been any major court challenges to the law establishing the PRLA? What were they based on?

29. Are there special procedures for disputes against the PRLA?

30. Have there been any major challenges of the method for determining "just compensation," as described in footnote 118, page 922?

31. Has the 15-year time limit on land reserved for public facilities (page 920, paragraph 1) presented any problems? Should the period be longer? Would a shorter period be sufficient?

FINANCIAL CONSIDERATIONS

32. What are the sources of funds and amounts to date for financing of the PRLA? (I have noted pages 920 and 921, which indicate that the PRLA can issue bonds and received an initial appropriation of $20 million.)

33. The article indicates (page 922, footnote 119) that $80 million has been used for acquisition to date and that $15.5 million has been "recouped from government agencies." How much of the remaining $64.5 million has been recouped through sales, rents, or other means, and what is the total debt of the PRLA?

34. Among the major criticisms of land banking in the literature is that local governments would lose real estate taxes on land acquired by a land-banking agency. Regarding taxes:
a. Does the PRLA pay local or other taxes on land acquired?
b. If the PRLA does not pay taxes, has a method of "payments in lieu of taxes" been devised?
c. If taxes or "payment in lieu of" are not made by the PRLA, has this an effect on local governmental units where the PRLA operates?

35. It has been hypothesized by some writers (particularly Marion Clawson) that the price of land not bought by a land-bank agency would rise and that the resultant increase in tax revenues would help offset the costs of the land-bank operation.

Is there any indication that this is happening in the San Juan metropolitan area in particular or in other areas of PRLA operations?

36. Clawson also identifies two other sources of possible gains through land banking. These are (a) savings in costs of public services where land development is more "compact" and (b) savings in the provision of public facilities, both in the service of developing areas and in the savings on land costs.

Are there indications that these savings are occurring in the San Juan metropolitan area in particular or in other areas of PRLA operations?

37. One of the primary functions generally identified for land banking and specifically for the PRLA (page 919, item d) is to reduce the high rate of land price rise. Further, on page 917, paragraph 2, it is stated that land prices rose at 20-30 percent yearly before establishment of the PRLA.

What effects has the PRLA had on the rate of land price rise in general? What is the approximate range of land price rise at present in areas where the PRLA operates relative to the 20-30 percent figure?

38. For land disposed of through sale, how does the disposal price compare with that of privately held land?

39. What are the basic characteristics of the methods used for determining the sale and rental prices for land disposal?

40. Land banking is often dismissed in the literature as too expensive to be practical. Considering the experience to date, including only costs and cost savings, has the PRLA experience proved economical? Has it required a substantial subsidy? (I recognize, of course, that there are other benefits of land banking, as I have outlined in earlier questions).

41. If the answer to Question 40 is generally negative, would a certain amount of additional funds—providing more dollars and more cost savings—make the PRLA economical?

STRUCTURE

42. What are the basic characteristics of the PRLA?

43. What is the relationship between the PRLA and local governments in the San Juan metropolitan area?

44. What is the relationship between the PRLA and the Puerto Rico Planning Board?

45. Is there a process for citizen involvement—direct or indirect—in the decisions of the PRLA in addition to representation by the governor and his appointees?

OVERVIEW—CONCLUSIONS

46. What are seen as the major accomplishments of the PRLA during its 13-year history?

47. Considering the special characteristics of Puerto Rico, what are the most important lessons for land banking in other localities that can be learned from the PRLA?

What conditions must be present to make land banking realistic elsewhere?

48. What additional characteristics would be desirable for the PRLA?

49. What significant problems and issues have been experienced by the PRLA?

50. Is it expected that a formal evaluation of the PRLA will be conducted in the near future?

51. What are the primary differences between the original expectations of the effects of the PRLA on metropolitan and Puerto Rico planning with the experience to date.

52. What influence have the changes in government had on the effectiveness of the PRLA and its relation to area planning?

53. What are the major techniques used for implementing the master plan for the San Juan metropolitan area?

BIBLIOGRAPHY

Advisory Commission on Intergovernmental Relations. Urban and Rural America: Policies for Future Growth (Washington, D.C., 1968).

American Institute of Architects. A Plan For Urban Growth: Report of the National Policy Task Force, 1972.

────── . Report of the Constraints Conference, 1973.

American Society of Planning Officials. Metropolitan Planning Policy Implementation, Planning Advisory Service Report no. 262 (Chicago, October 1970).

────── . Increasing State and Regional Power in the Development Process, Planning Advisory Service Report no. 255 (Chicago, March 1970).

Bab, Herbert J. G. "New Policies to Control Land Use in Hawaii" (unpublished draft), chap. 3.

Bosselman, Fred P. Alternatives to Urban Sprawl: Legal Guidelines for Governmental Action, Research Report no. 15 (Washington, D.C.: The National Commission on Urban Problems, 1968).

Bowman, Labarbara. "Montgomery Acts to Cut Growth," Washington Post, 27 June 1973, p. C1, cols. 6-8, p. C8, cols 1-3.

Callies, David L. "Commonwealth of Puerto Rico v. Rosso: Land Banking and an Expanded Concept of Public Use," Land-Use Controls: A Quarterly Review 2 (1968): 17-31.

Center for Urban Development Research. Public Land Acquisition for New Communities and the Control of Urban Growth: Alternative Strategies, final report prepared for the New York State Urban Development Corporation (Ithaca, N.Y.: Cornell University, March 1973).

Clawson, Marion. Suburban Land Conversion in the United States: An Economic and Governmental Process (Baltimore, Md.: The Johns Hopkins Press, 1971).

Crane, Jacob L. Urban Planning—Illusion and Reality (New York: Vantage press, 1973).

Downs, Anthony. "Alternative Forms of Future Urban Growth in the United States," JAIP 36, no. 1 (January 1970): 3-11.

Duckworth, Robert P., et al. Development Corporations, Open Space and Implementation Tools Project, Maryland-National Capital Park and Planning Commission, 1968.

_____. The Land Reserves System: An Approach to the Possible Application to the Bi-County Region, Working Paper no. 13, (Maryland-National Capital Park and Planning Commission, 1968).

Edwards, Gordon. Land, People and Policy (West Trenton, N.J.: Chandler Davis, 1969).

Fairfax County Office of Research and Statistics, Feasibility of Land Banking in Fairfax County: A Preliminary Study (Fairfax County, Va., June 29, 1973).

Fishman, Richard P., and Gross, Robert D. "Note, Public Land Banking: A New Praxis For Urban Growth" (23 Case W. Res. Law Rev. 897, 1972).

Hartke, Vance. "Toward a National Growth Policy"(22 Catholic Univ. L. Rev. 231, 1973).

Hawaii Senate, Ways and Means Committee. A Bill for an Act Establishing a State Development Corporation and Land Bank, 7th Legislature, 1973 (S.B. No. 1350).

Heeter, David. Toward a More Effective Land Use Guidance System: A Summary and Analysis of Five Major Reports, Planning Advisory Service Report no. 250 (Chicago, Ill.: American Society of Planning Officials, 1969).

Hussman, William H. Memorandum to County Manager: Advance Land Acquisition and Land Bank (Montgomery County, Md.: Office of Program Coordination, 1968).

Jordan, Fred. "Land Speculation in the Public Interest," City 1 (January-February 1971): 85-86.

Kamm, Sylvan. Land Availability for Housing and Urban Growth (Washington, D.C.: The Urban Institute, 1970).

_____. Land Banking: Public Policy Alternatives and Dilemmas (Washington, D.C.: The Urban Institute, 1970).

_____. Reducing Land Costs Through Improvements in the Market Mechanism: A Potential System of Land Exchange Banks (Washington, D.C.: The Urban Institute, 1970).

Kramer, Ann. "A Proposed Land Bank System for Maryland" (mimeographed outline). 1968.

Maryland Planning and Zoning Law Study Commission. "A Review and Discussion of Development Trends in Maryland," Interim Report, January 1968.

_____. Legislative Recommendations, Final Report, December 1969.

Maryland Senate. Public Facilities Area Development Act, 1968, secs. 26A-1, 26A-4 Montgomery County Code.

Metropolitan Washington Council of Governments, Department of Regional Planning. Advance Land Acquisition: Concepts, Procedures and Potentials (Washington, D.C., 1968).

_____. The Changing Region (Washington, D.C., 1969).

Milgram, Grace. The City Expands, A Study of the Conversion of Land from Rural to Urban Use, Philadelphia 1945-62 (Philadelphia: University of Pennsylvania, 1967).

Milwaukee Buys Land for Reserve," New York Times, 1 April 1973, p. 88, col. 1.

Milwaukee Department of City Development. The Land Bank: Eight Years of Industrial Development Progress 1964-1971, Report to the Common Councils Committee on Economic Development (Milwaukee, Wis., March 1972).

Milwaukee Division of Economic Development. Report of the Ad Hoc Advisory Committee on Land Use Strategies Concerning Industrial Development Policies and Programs for the 1970's (Milwaukee, Wis., October 1972).

National Commission on Urban Problems. Building The American City (Washington, D.C., 1968).

_____. Fragmentation in Land Use Planning and Controls, Research Report no. 18 (Washington, D.C., 1969).

New Jersey Senate. S.B. No. 803, May 12, 1969. Introduced by
Senators Willard B. Knowlton and Richard J. Coffee.

Passow, Shirley S. "Land Reserves and Teamwork in Planning Stockholm," JAIP 36 (May 1970): 179-188.

Piedmont Triad Council of Governments. Land Bank Handbook (Greensboro, N.C., September 1972). Carol Van Alstyne, Ed.

Regional Planning Council. A Land Bank for the Baltimore Region, a Suggested Approach for Implementing the Regional Plan (Baltimore, Md., June 1967).

Reps, John W. "The Future of American Planning—Requiem or Renascence?" Land Use Controls 1, no. 2 (1967): 1-16.

Schmid, Allan A. "Suburban Land Appreciation and Public Policy," JAIP 36 no. 1 (January 1970): 38-43.

Shoup, Donald C., and Mack, Ruth P. Advance Land Acquisition by Local Governments (New York: Institute of Public Administration, 1968).

Subcommittee on Implementation of the Economic Development Loan Fund. Establishing a Non-Profit Corporation to Administer the $3 Million Economic Development Bond Fund, Report to the Mayor's Council of Economic Advisors (Baltimore, Md., 1972).

Sussna, Stephen. Land Use Controls, More Effective Approaches, Research Monograph no. 17 (Washington, D.C.: The Urban Institute, 1970).

Urban Land Research Analysts Corp. Investment Policy for Land Banks, Monograph no. 4 (Lexington, Mass., 1967).

_____. Land Banks for Planning and Control: Some General Principles and a Specific Application, Monograph no. 2 (Lexington, Mass., 1967).

_____. Measuring the Impact of Land Bank Policies on the Urban Land Market, Monograph no. 5 (Lexington, Mass., 1968).

_____. Municipal Land Banks: Land Reserve Policy for Urban Development (Lexington, Mass., October 1969).

_____. Municipal Land Reserves Policy: An Analytical Study of Foreign Experience, Monograph no. 6 (Lexington, Mass., 1968).

_____. The Determination of Urban Land Use and Land Values, Monograph no. 3 (Lexington, Mass., 1967).

_____. Toward Efficient Programs of Land use Controls (Lexington, Mass., 1969).

U.S. Department of Housing and Urban Development, Office of International Affairs. Urban Land Policy—Selected Aspects of European Experience (Washington, D.C. 1969).

_____. Office of Resources Development. Advance Acquisition of Land Application Log for 1969-1970 (Washington, D.C., 1970).

U.S. Congress, House, Committee on Banking and Currency, Subcommittee on Housing Panels, papers Harr, Charles M. Wanted: Two Federal Levers for Urban Land Use—Land Banks and Urbank, June 1971, pp. 927-940.

_____, papers Kamm, Sylvan. Land Availability for Housing and Urban Growth, June 1971, pp. 263-286.

_____, Senate, Committee on Government Operation. S. 1286, A Bill to Provide for National Growth Policy Planning, and for Other Purposes, 93d Cong., 1st sess., March 19, 1973.

_____, Joint Economic Committee, Subcommittee on Economic Progress. A Proposal for Achieving Balanced National Growth and Development, 93d Cong., 1st sess., 1973.

Wilhelm, Paul A. "Industrial Development Planning," JAIP 26 (August 1960): 216-223.

ABOUT THE AUTHOR

HARVEY L. FLECHNER is a Principal Planner with the Indianapolis Department of Metropolitan Development. Previously he was with the Metropolitan Washington Council of Governments and the urban and transportation planning consultant firm Barton-Aschman Associates.

Mr. Flechner received his M.A. in City and Regional Planning from the Catholic University of America and B.S. in Civil Engineering from the City College of New York.

RELATED TITLES
Published by
Praeger Special Studies

AIR QUALITY MANAGEMENT AND LAND USE
PLANNING: Legal, Administrative, and
Methodological Perspectives
      George Hagevik, Daniel R. Mandelker,
      and Richard K. Brail

COMMUNITY DEVELOPMENT STRATEGIES:
Case Studies of Major Model Cities
      George J. Washnis

EXCLUSIONARY ZONING: Land Use Regulation
and Housing in the 1970s
      Richard F. Babcock and
      Fred P. Bosselman

IMPACT OF FEDERAL LEGISLATION AND
PROGRAMS ON PRIVATE LAND IN
URBAN AND METROPOLITAN DEVELOPMENT
      Joseph L. Stevens

PLANNING FOR URBAN GROWTH:
British Perspectives on the Planning Process
      Edited by John L. Taylor

THE POLITICAL REALITIES OF URBAN
URBAN PLANNING
      Don T. Allensworth

THE POLITICS OF LAND USE: Planning,
Zoning, and the Private Developer
      R. Robert Linowes and
      Don T. Allensworth